"With warmth, clarity, and humor, Irini Rockwell brings to life traditional Tibetan Buddhist teachings on the inner energies that activate and color our experience. Following her teacher, the great meditation master Chögyam Trungpa, Rockwell shows how these teachings touch the living heart of our personal styles, as well as our relationships with others and our environment."

—JEREMY HAYWARD, author of *Sacred World* and *Perceiving Ordinary Magic*

"*The Five Wisdom Energies* reflects Irini Rockwell's passionate and unique vision of the five buddha families. She offers a delightful and practical manual for understanding and working with self and other."

—KAREN KISSEL WEGELA, Ph.D., author of *How to Be a Help Instead of a Nuisance* and longtime leader of five-wisdom-energy programs through Naropa University

THE FIVE WISDOM ENERGIES

A Buddhist Way of Understanding

Personalities, Emotions, and Relationships

IRINI ROCKWELL

SHAMBHALA
Boston & London
2002

Shambhala Publications, Inc.
Horticultural Hall
300 Massachusetts Avenue
Boston, Massachusetts 02115
www.shambhala.com

9 8 7 6 5 4 3 2 1

First Edition
Printed in the United States of America

⊚ This edition is printed on acid-free paper that meets
the American National Standards Institute Z39.48 Standard.
Distributed in the United States by Random House, Inc.,
and in Canada by Random House of Canada Ltd

Library of Congress Cataloging-in-Publication Data
Rockwell, Irini Nadel.
The five wisdom energies : a Buddhist way of understanding personalities,
emotions, and relationships / Irini Rockwell.—1st ed.
p.   cm.
Includes bibliographical references and index.
ISBN 1-57062-451-8
1. Spiritual life—Buddhism.   2. Buddhism—China—Tibet.   I. Title.
BQ7805.R63 2002
294.3'422—dc21   2001049555

TO

CHÖGYAM TRUNGPA RINPOCHE

CONTENTS

IV. FIVE STYLES OF RELATING TO OTHERS

APPENDIXES

ACKNOWLEDGMENTS

This book weaves together my work with contemplative approaches to working in psychotherapy, education, organizations, and the arts. It would never have come into being without the help of a great many people in many walks of life.

First, I would like to express my tremendous appreciation for Chögyam Trungpa Rinpoche, who introduced me to a world where I can simultaneously embrace who I am and let go of who I am. His teachings on meditation, psychology, the arts, and simply becoming a full human being have been the primary inspiration for my life and this book. Trungpa Rinpoche always encouraged us to experiment in working with the buddha-family energies. He listened to people's suggestions and trusted their experiences and insights. I always felt he was giving me an open, fertile field in which to play. For this I am deeply grateful. My heartfelt thanks also go to his son Sakyong Mipham Rinpoche, who has been so immensely supportive and encouraging of the Maitri work in general and this book in particular. In addition, over the last ten years, the teachings of Khenpo Tsultrim Gyamtso have been a powerful force in my life. His spontaneous presence, profound teachings, and playful energy give me great inspiration and joy.

I would also like to thank my family. My husband, John Rockwell, posted slogans like "Never give up on maitri," "Love to the maitri lady," and "Drive all maitri into oneself" at just the right times to give me a boost of warm, playful encouragement. I am thankful to my children, who, in so fully being who they are, have inspired me. My son, Julian, with whom I have talked about the energies all his life, continually inspires me with how he uses his understanding of the energies, whether in teaching kids at risk, in his intimate relationships, or more recently with organizational development work. I love the directness with which my daughter, Chandra, reveals herself and explores her world through the energies. Most touching has been my father's response to reading some of this manuscript. It precipitated a closeness between us that we had never before experienced so fully. At age eighty-two he was so inspired that he presented some of these ideas to a Quaker forum to which he belongs.

To the many others who inspired me, influenced me, and supported me as the book unfolded, I express much appreciation. As the person who was the initial catalyst for this book, I would like to thank Martha Bonzi, who put it into my head that I could do this. I would like to acknowledge the many teachers of Shambhala Buddhism and especially of five wisdom energies work, the participants in programs, my students, my clients, and members of the Maitri Council International. They teach me continually and have helped me evolve my personal understanding over the past twenty-five years. In particular I have explored this work at many levels and have formed deep friendships and close working relationships with many teachers of the energies. I would like to thank Marvin Casper, Ed Podvoll, Jeff Fortuna, Karen Kissel Wegela, Susan Skjei, Judy Lief, Pema Chödrön, Allyn Lyon, John Rockwell, Claudette Rodrigue, Melissa Moore, Paul Cashman, and Jeremy Hayward for sharing their insights and experiences with me. Many thanks to Claudette for contributions to the activities for the energies.

I want to acknowledge with much appreciation those individuals and organizations that have been financially supportive throughout the years it has taken to write the book: Ernst Leibhardt, Nancy Edison, and the Nalanda Individual Assistance Trust.

Most important, I wish to thank Emily Hilburn Sell, my editor at Shambhala Publications, who provided the essential nurturing as well as critical feedback that brought this material to the world in written form. Without her I could not have endured the laborious process of translating this work into contemporary language for general understanding. It has been a special pleasure to work with the Shambhala Publications staff: Jonathan Green, Emily Bower, Susan Cohan, and Peter Bermudes. Their expertise has been an inspiration. This process was much aided by the work of several others who assisted with editing: Holly Hammond, to whom I am indebted for clarifying the material with a major line editing; Laura Perrault, whose infectious enthusiasm to work on the book came at just the right moment; my ex-husband Ernie Nadel, who gave some very helpful editing suggestions; and finally my son, Julian, who added his own insights and flavor in several parts as icing on the cake.

PART ONE

FIVE WISDOM ENERGIES

1

Discovering Energy

MY STORY

One summer day in 1976, I was sitting in a friend's apartment in Boulder, Colorado, where we were both assistant teaching at Naropa University, a school that focuses on training in the arts, Buddhism, and contemplative psychotherapy. Naropa's founder, the Tibetan meditation master Chögyam Trungpa, had written a book called *Cutting Through Spiritual Materialism*, which I was reading. The following passage caught my eye: "In the Tantric tradition energy is categorized in five basic qualities or Buddha Families: Vajra, Ratna, Padma, Karma and Buddha. Each Buddha family has an emotion associated with it which is transmuted into a particular 'wisdom' or aspect of the awakened state of mind. The Buddha families are also associated with colors, elements, landscapes, directions, seasons, with any aspect of the phenomenal world."

Reading those words aligned me with my world. It confirmed many feelings and experiences that I had had in my life. Though I had not yet begun to practice sitting meditation and knew almost nothing about contemplative traditions, somehow I instinctively knew about the energies of which he wrote.

My immediate connection came from my life as a dancer, choreographer, and teacher. I was passionately interested in examining the dynamic qualities of expressive movement. For example, I had choreographed a piece about animals called "In Wildness," which explored how a prairie dog moves in contrast to a deer, how the energy of a flock of birds contrasts with the feeling of a lion coming in for the kill. In other dances I explored human emotions—the heat of love, the strength of anger, the stiffness of pride, the sparkle of joy.

Reading Chögyam Trungpa's words that day changed my life. It led me to a contemplative tradition with an understanding of energy at its core that acknowledged the inherent sanity and richness of my art discipline—and life—while allowing me to step onto a meditative path. For the next few years, the five Buddha families increasingly became part of my dance work. As they did, my awareness of these energies began to color my perspective in other aspects of my life, particularly my relationships with people. Why was it that one man brought out my intellectual curiosity and another my physical desire? Why did I feel at ease with one person and anxious with another? Why would I feel powerful in one situation but inhibited and frustrated in another? What was the energetic relationship between myself, these people, and these situations?

Seven years later I was able to begin working with the practice associated with the five energies—that of taking postures in colored environments to heighten their qualities. (See appendix B, "Maitri Programs.") At that time I staffed a three-month program in which people practiced like this in depth. Meanwhile, I had become the director of undergraduate dance and dance therapy at Naropa. I was seeing dance students become extremely self-conscious about their creative work when they began to practice meditation. It dawned on me that to hear the message "Be who you are," which the five wisdom energies work had brought home for me, might also be helpful for them. Gradually I introduced energies work into the dance curriculum.

When I realized that I had become more interested in my students as people than as artists, I took a degree in contemplative psychotherapy and worked as a therapist. As my work with the five energies evolved, I became more interested in group dynamics and moved into organizational development work and education. Today I train, consult, facilitate, and coach with the five energies work for health professionals, leaders in organizations, educators in schools, artists, and private clients. In writing this book, I drew from the teachings of Buddhist master Chögyam Trungpa Rinpoche and from my own experience and understanding, which is reflected in the examples, images, and exercises.

THE FIVE WISDOM ENERGIES

The five wisdom energies pervade our very being, our interactions with others, and every aspect of the phenomenal world. They manifest in posture, emotional tones, and personality types as well as in landscapes, seasons, and environments. Each energy style expresses itself in some personality traits that we commonly classify as dysfunctional or neurotic and in some that we consider constructive or wise. Both troublesome emotions and pleasant ones arise out of this energetic matrix.

The energies are easily identified by their colors, which hold the essence of their qualities. Just as light radiates, so does energy. The color of energy is like colored light. The following descriptions of the five energy families capture their colors as well as both their wisdom and their confusion:

- The *vajra family* reflects a blue energy like a crystal-clear mirror. Vajra energy reflects what it sees without bias; this is its wisdom quality. It also has a self-righteousness that can harden into cold or hot anger; that is its confused quality.
- The *ratna family* exudes a rich and earthy golden yellow energy that encompasses everything. The wisdom quality of ratna energy is richness, equanimity, and satisfaction. But it can also turn into greedy territoriality and puffed-up pride, which is its neurotic quality.

- The *padma family* glows with the vitality of red energy. Padma energy's passion is, at its best, compassionate wisdom. At its neurotic worst, it manifests as grasping. In its wisdom it is finely tuned in to what is happening, discriminating experience without bias. However, when it is neurotic, it can cling obsessively to what gives pleasure.
- The *karma family* emits a green energy, swift and energetic like the wind. Karma energy is all-accomplishing action for the benefit of others; this is its wisdom quality. It can also become power-hungry, manipulative, competitive, and envious; that is its confused quality.
- The *buddha family* radiates a white energy, spacious and peaceful. Buddha energy is an all-pervasive, peaceful space; this is its wisdom quality. It can also be solidly immobile with the density of ignoring or denying; that is its confused quality.

In five energies work we often talk as if people were one type or another. Thus I refer to "vajra people" and "padma people." However, although certain individuals may manifest a particular family vividly, it is probably more accurate to say that Rebecca displays a lot of vajra energy than to say that she's a vajra person. Although someone's style of behavior might display one particular energy clearly, the other energies are always at play. It takes awareness, time, and practice to really understand the full range of energies within ourselves. We are all very colorful.

As in any good novel, the people and their circumstances in this book are fictitious. Their stories are based on what I have observed, and sometimes I have simplified them to make a point.

ORIGINS: A PRACTICE FOR WESTERNERS

In the early 1970s Chögyam Trungpa Rinpoche introduced a way of approaching the five wisdom energies, traditionally known as the five Buddha families, that made them accessible to non-Buddhists. His great friend and spiritual colleague Zen teacher Shunryo Suzuki Roshi was involved with the initial idea. The two of them observed that some people, especially those who were emotionally disturbed or confused, found traditional Buddhist sitting meditation difficult. They thought of creating a community where such people could live together and practice. The question was, what practice would they do? Unfortunately Suzuki Roshi died before the seeds of their discussion could bear fruit. But something was soon to happen to Trungpa Rinpoche that gave him an idea for putting their original inspiration into practice.

While teaching a residential program in a hotel, Trungpa attended a party one night in someone's room. One person was creating a scene—singing and dancing, trying to get everyone else to join in. As the energy became more and more intense, Rinpoche felt the room becoming claustrophobic. Suddenly he realized that, in fact, they were in a box—four walls, ceiling, floor—and that the box was becoming colored by a particular energy. It reminded him of a traditional Tibetan Buddhist retreat practice using a small room in total darkness.

Shortly after that evening Rinpoche started drawing diagrams of rooms. Eventually he designed five rooms, each with its own color and window shape. In each room the student would lie in a specific posture. The combination of space, color, and posture evoked and intensified one of the five basic energy patterns. The process of taking a specific posture in a specific room would allow the student to work through that particular neurosis and find the wisdom and sanity inherent in that energy.

Thus Maitri Space Awareness™ practice—"Maitri" for short—was born. The word *maitri* in Sanskrit means openness and friendliness. Space refers to the total environment—not just of the room but also of the world at large. Space is the totality of experience. It includes everything in our sphere: what we think, see, feel, hear, touch. Awareness is our attentiveness to what is happening in that space.

It was part of Trungpa Rinpoche's genius to present esoteric tantric teachings in an immediate and direct way that was accessible to anyone. With Maitri Space Awareness practice, anyone can experience and transform the energies of the five Buddha families. So although this practice is presented as a contemplative discipline, it is not presented in a traditional Buddhist format. (For further information see appendix B, "Maitri Programs," and appendix C, "Places to Practice Meditation and Maitri.")

LEVELS OF UNDERSTANDING

When we begin to become aware of the energies, we see how our patterns of behavior, emotions, intellect, and temperament correspond to one or more of the five families. This awareness can become the foundation for developing a practical way of working with ourselves, others, and the phenomenal world. It's not that we'll filter every minute of our day through the perspective of the five colors. However, we will find that some situations become clear and workable only when we connect to their energetic dynamic.

My children, Julian and Chandra, have been brought up on the five wisdom energies. As a result they better understand many aspects of their lives: their own style, their relationships with others, where they feel at home. They talk about the energies of their friends, teachers, and work colleagues. They also enjoy observing people's styles in movies and books. They are attuned to environments and how they react to them: earthy, more ratna Chandra loves to live in the country and care for animals; fun-loving, speedy padma/karma Julian loves cities. His padma passion dramas over the years have given us occasion for many a conversation about the energetic patterns of relationships.

The importance of developing a sense of loving-kindness—maitri—toward ourselves plays a big part in working with the five wisdom energies. It is a universal truth that we all want to love and be loved. Yet what we often miss in desperately seeking love from others or loving blindly without reserve is that what we most need is to love ourselves. It is only when we love ourselves that we can love others; it is through loving ourselves that we become lovable. No matter how many times we hear it or from whom, this message is all too easy to forget.

Loving ourselves has to do with accepting, relaxing, opening, and feeling warmth. Even as I write and remember this, I feel the tension in my body unwinding; I feel gentler toward myself. As I open to myself, I feel gentler toward others as well. The space provided by relaxing my body allows me to open to my sense perceptions. Looking out my window, I see that it is a beautiful day; I almost missed it. Gentleness toward myself feels peaceful. I notice that I breathe more deeply and easily. I am no longer struggling against myself or what's around me. I feel comforted by the openness of my own heart. This nourishment is coming from within. This is maitri.

Working with maitri in the context of the five energies is a way of tuning in to the energetic quality of life. When we experience loving-kindness, we allow ourselves to feel the energies without holding back; we have the potential to be brilliantly sane. With maitri we see that we and the world are fundamentally good. Maitri allows us to make friends with ourselves and our world.

Five energies work is based on the premise that fundamentally we are good, sane, intelligent people. When we experience a sense of well-being, we know that, however bad we sometimes feel about ourselves, our sanity is intrinsic, fundamental. We discover that we accept more fully who we are and engage genuinely with every aspect of our lives. The unconditional friendliness of maitri is the key to the most powerful aspect of working with the five energies: transforming neurosis into wisdom.

As a frequent flier, I never cease to be amazed that up there, above the clouds, the sun is always shining—twenty-four hours a day. Too often we forget this, see only the clouds, and become convinced that they are real. We make the clouds solid and identify with them. However, with maitri we can begin to see the clouds as transparent and illusory. In fact, we can fly right through them, though the ride might get a little bumpy. When we identity with the sun, we are touching our intrinsic sanity. It is characterized by openness, clarity, and compassion.

Knowing what the five energies are is only the beginning. To experience their transformative power, you need to tune in to them daily, refining your sensitivity and understanding. Direct experience speaks louder than words. So, please, jump in. This book requires your input, your engagement. Working with the five wisdom energies is not academic; it's experiential. The approaches offered here are intended to guide your experience, drawing it out as well as elucidating it. They encompass three stages: learning, contemplating, and embodying. In the learning stage, the five energies and ideas around them remain somewhat conceptual. In the contemplating stage, you start to feel affinity with the energies as part of who you are and spontaneously use them as a reference point. At the embodying stage, they become both psychologically and physically integrated, and there is no separation between what you understand intellectually and how you live.

BASIC PREMISES

What we will explore in this book is grounded in the following fundamental understandings:

- Energy is the basic vitality of our existence—the quality, texture, ambiance, and tone of both the animate and the inanimate.
- Becoming familiar with the five energies that pervade all aspects of our existence opens the door to a subtle level of being.
- Energy is an experience, not something we can understand conceptually.
- Through our thoughts and emotions, we experience the energy of our inner world; through our sense perceptions (seeing, hearing, smelling, tasting, and touching), we experience the outer world.

- Energy is neutral; our attitude toward it is what determines whether we are open (sane) or closed (confused).
- Emotions—whether in their sane or confused aspects—are a vivid display of energy.
- We each have certain energetic styles, which intensify when life pushes our buttons.
- The point at which our energy is negatively intensified is the most opportune time to work with it because that is when we experience the energy most vividly.
- When our energy is stuck over a period of time, we experience an imbalance in our psychophysical being, leading to mental and/or physical illness.
- Regaining our sense of energetic well-being comes from working directly with energy.
- An attitude of unconditional friendliness, maitri, toward whatever arises in our being is the catalyst for turning our energy around.
- Wisdom energy—the inseparability of confusion and sanity—is spacious and brilliant.
- When we manifest our wisdom, we align ourselves with the totality of the five energies and ride the energy of the moment.
- When we are in tune with the energies, we experience our connection to everyone and everything in an energetic matrix, the mandala.
- When we have a sense of how to work with energetic reality, we can creatively apply our understanding anywhere, anytime, no matter what we are doing.

In writing about the five wisdom energies, I hope to give you an introduction to a way of working with yourself that has the potential to profoundly transform your life. The five wisdom energies are an invitation to dance your own dance, sing your own song, all within the vivid display of the mandala, the energetic sphere. Knowing them is an invitation to create your world and work compassionately with people. Most of all, it is an invitation to ride the energy of the moment and celebrate its brilliance. I hope you will be inspired to discover for yourself the richness of living in a multicolored world. This book is like a finger pointing at a rainbow; the energies are the rainbow itself.

EXERCISES: AWARENESS

This exercise is designed to bring you into the world of energy. You will get the most out of this exercise by trying it when you can be very attentive to what is going on around you.

When you're with a group of people you know well—your family, housemates, or colleagues—sit quietly and, without looking at them, see whether you can discriminate among different people's energies. What are their colors? Their textures? As you do this, sense perceptions other than sight will come into play and give you clues. These other sense perceptions might tell you more about your friends than if you looked at them directly. Next, try the same thing with someone with whom you're having an emotional upheaval. Drop your concepts about what is going on between you and see whether you can experience your energy patterns and those of the other person.

You can also try sensing energies in different environments. Go into the various rooms of your house and feel the energy. How is the kitchen different from the living room? the bedroom? How is the energy different in an airport than in a candy store? at a party? in a school? How do you react? Do you push certain situations away and gravitate toward others? Can you take the environment as your partner and dance with it?

If you were a food, what type of food would you be? Describe yourself. As that food, what other food would you like best? That is, if you were a potato, would you like to be friends with a hot dog? an artichoke? a plum? Describe the energy of your food friend. What do you two have to say to each other? Could you play together, or would you end up fighting? You can also play this game with elements, flowers, landscapes, cars, and so on.

2

Where in the World Is Energy?

One morning I was listening to the classical music station. The announcer introducing Beethoven's Fifth Symphony was lamenting how many words had been spoken trying to explain the meaning of this powerful piece of music. Finally he said, "It's just pure energy! Pure Beethoven!" I burst out laughing as I realized that he was essentially urging people to get beyond their concepts and connect directly with the power of the music. Yes!

The world we perceive, conceptualize, and think we know is only a surface reality. Underneath it lies a magical realm, more elusive and yet more vivid. Every philosophical, spiritual, and religious tradition, every art form, in every corner of the globe, in every century of human existence, teaches about this deeper reality. In this book we refer to it as the surprising and powerful force called energy. To move through the world without connecting to energy is like learning about being in love from reading romance novels. Just as we don't really know love until we love, so we are not truly in the world until we engage with it energetically.

Energy is the vibrant aspect of being—the quality, texture, ambience, and tone of both the animate and the inanimate, the visible and the invisible. It is the basic vitality of our existence. It pervades our inner, psychological world as well as the outer, phenomenal world. It exists in what we see, smell, taste, touch, hear, and feel. People express their energy through attitudes, emotions, decisions, and actions. Furthermore, we each display energy in our own unique ways—through body posture, facial expressions, mannerisms, word choices, the tone and tempo of our voice.

Energy is life force, our natural power or strength. It resides in our breathing. When our breathing changes, our emotions change, our movements change, and our perception of the world changes accordingly. When our vital energy is obscured by strong emotions, opinions, and concepts, our perspective narrows and our strength diminishes. When we are free of such blockages, our power is free and expansive.

From moment to moment our experience is made of bodily sensations, feelings, thoughts, and perceptions. We string these myriad and constantly shifting elements together to create what we call "I" and "my experience" and "the world." For example, when we eat an apple, we see it, touch it, taste it, and then decide whether we like it. Altogether this is our "apple-eating experience." When we are not bound by the solid sense of self that comes from building a story line or making our experiences into an identity, we can connect with our innate energy. Without the filters, the energetic quality of our existence is more fluid, fragmented, illusory, and shimmering. With no solid sense of "me" to block the flow, it is pleasurable to experience ourselves.

Energy is also a way of understanding karma, the Buddhist view of cause and result. The energetic makeup of a situation produces (causes) a corresponding energetic situation (result). Our thoughts, words, and actions have their inevitable outcome. Traditional Buddhism sees that these patterns follow us through lifetimes and so create our karma, good or bad. Working with ourselves, our energy, is the key to creating good karma.

The forces of nature are elemental energy in the raw. Earth is solid, firm, and trustworthy, a good foundation and a nourishing ground. Water is fluid, changeable: it can be forceful and flowing or still and reflective. Fire is playful and intense, quixotic and passionate, impossible to grasp. Air might manifest as a light, refreshing breeze, which seems harmonious, or as a harsh hurricane.

Elemental energy is harder to experience in cities, where we fortify ourselves against the elements by creating constructs, much as we fortify ourselves against energetic reality by creating story lines. We confine earth to potted plants and manicured gardens; water to sinks, bathtubs, and toilet bowls; fire to the fireplace and stove; and air to fans, vents, and air conditioners. There is nothing wrong with this, though domesticating the elements tends to distance us from their magic.

We can evoke energy through creative expression. For example, in an autobiographical dance theater piece, I moved through many different emotional states, focusing not on specific life events but on their emotional energy. In pounding a hanging duffel bag (as a boxer would) and repeating the line "Could, would, should, go do" until it became a screech, I evoked a masculine energy. The feelings I had about my mother's dying took the emotional energy of the query "Mother, why did you die on me?" and turned into a cry as I ran across the stage. The experience of the evoked energy had more impact than the words.

We can also see people as manifestations of different energies. Imagine for a moment that good friends walk into your living room. Instead of seeing them as the Jenny or Steve you "know" so well, erase your familiar picture of them and notice their energetic qualities. See a perky, fun-loving, fluidly moving Jenny. See a slow-moving Steve, with a soft smile and accommodating manner, who never gets ruffled. Both are expressing their particular energies—their quality, tone, and rhythm; their dance; their song.

Most of the time we think of the physical world as composed of solid material, yet it also has an energetic aspect. A table is a "table." We rarely notice the energy the table radiates. A shiny, smooth table radiates a different energy than an old, beat-up table. The big thing in the yard that has roots, a trunk, branches, and leaves—we call it a tree. We know a few things about tables and trees. Yet naming things and having concepts about them is different from experiencing them on an energetic level.

In new environments we are more likely to be aware of the reality of energy because we have fewer preexisting ideas through which to filter our immediate perceptions. Awareness is heightened further if we are unfamiliar with the language, because we are less apt to get distracted by words. I once traveled by train through a long tunnel in the Alps that took us from German Switzerland into Italian Switzerland. Although at the time I didn't know what had changed, I felt the difference in my surroundings vividly and immediately after emerging from the tunnel. I knew with my whole being that I was in a different energy space, a different ambience. The air became soft and warm, colors were brighter, and my body relaxed. The freshness of my sense perceptions connected me with the people and the place.

Providing the right ambient energy for a situation can enhance it. A language school in Minnesota exemplifies this by creating different "villages" for each language taught there. Each village is a miniature replica of a country, with the appropriate architecture, food, and so forth. People learn more easily because the language is evoked by the energy of the surroundings.

To illustrate: I spent my early childhood years in Turkey. When I was eight and my sister was ten, we took a two-year sabbatical in the States. Upon returning to Turkey on the boat, my sister and I realized we had completely forgotten our Turkish. Dad's lessons on deck made no impact. The end of our journey came; the boat neared the port of Istanbul. It eased up to the dock, and the walkway was placed. Our Turkish friends came running up to us, crying out warm greetings. And down we ran to them, answering in perfectly fluent Turkish, completely oblivious to the fact that our language memories had returned!

All world cultures have found ways to explore, celebrate, and express energetic reality in their religions, art, and philosophical traditions. In Greek and Roman mythology as well as in Eastern religions such as Buddhism, Hinduism, and Shinto, different deities symbolize different energies. In vajrayana Buddhism the five wisdom energies are traditionally presented as the five Buddha families and are personified as symbolic deities. As such they have been around for over a thousand years. Native Americans recognize elemental energies as spirits. Buddhists and Hindus evoke particular energies by chanting mantras, repetitions of certain sounds or words. African and Australian peoples use ritual dance to call up energies or spirits.

Whether in art or science or religion, a cultural conceptual overlay can block our experience of the energy. Symbols lose their power because we objectify them. For instance, in objectifying energies as religious deities, we can forget the relevance of their innate energy to everyday life. We think of them as separate from ourselves. In my experience as a practitioner of vajrayana Buddhism, however, I have found that it is possible, by understanding the five Buddha families as elemental energies, to close the gap between their symbolic representation and our experience.

Novelists, musicians, painters, dancers, and poets all tune in to the world of energy in their art. Music expresses a full range of energies, from the pizzicato of violins to the rhythm of drums to the driving beat of a rock guitar. Classical ballet, European folk dance, and slam dancing each evoke a unique energy. In visual art the impressionistic canvases of Monet and van Gogh display an energy quite different from the abstractions of Mondrian or Klee. The works of art that come to be considered classic are often those that most gracefully and powerfully evoke the universal energies and communicate them to their audience.

Sciences like acupuncture and feng shui and body disciplines like martial arts and hatha yoga work specifically with energy as a medium of healing. These disciplines are based on working with the meridians, or energy channels of the body. The basic principle is that our energy moves along certain lines, but in the course of life, particularly when we are ill, the energy becomes blocked. Acupuncture or postures that work with energy are ways to unblock this energy. Psychology has noted the importance of energy in body-centered therapies like bioenergetics. Cognitive science and the study of perception bring the physical and psychological worlds together through theories about energy.

Energy can be used to enhance function, as athletes and dancers know well. Watch the swings, falls, jumps of a gymnast and see how they align with energy. As a dancer, I often found that if I focused only on the technical aspects of a movement—lifting my leg above my head, turning on one leg with my body arched back, leaping across the room—the move was difficult. When I connected with the energy of what I was doing, the movement was easier and more enjoyable. I would use an image—reaching my leg to the sky, rooting my supporting leg in the earth as I threw my body into the turn, and then experiencing myself as weightless as air on the jump.

Feeling is a word that we use for both physical and mental experiences. Feeling joins body and mind. It is more complex than the physical pain we get from banging our knee. It is more subtle than an emotion like anger, or thoughts about what we have to do tomorrow. Feeling is like a sixth sense, the ability to tune in intuitively to what is happening. It joins intellect and intuition, heart and mind. It is the way we experience energy.

A colloquial language acknowledging the power of energy has grown up since the 1960s, when we might have heard people talk about energy as vibrations, as in "picking up the vibes" of a person or place. The verb *grok* came into being; it means to understand the full situation intuitively. When we "grok" something, we pick up the "vibe" in a way that transcends concepts. Nowadays we might say that a person has "presence" or a place has "atmosphere." An event might be characterized as "intense" or a person as "mellow." These terms simply acknowledge that each person and situation has a perceivable energy.

Working with energy plugs us into our experience in a way that reveals its illusory nature as well as the illusory nature of the world around us. We see that the world is not as solid as it seems; it is made up of energies constantly in flux. There is nothing, yet there is something. For instance, a favorite view in a natural setting is infinitely changeable, depending on the time of day, the seasons, the weather. There is no one view. We could hardly say it is the same place in February as it is in August. And so it is with our bodies, the elements of which have come together in a form that we call "human," which will dissolve when we die.

3

Our Psychophysical Barometer

In this chapter we will look at becoming a psychophysical barometer. Having seen the energetic possibilities in our world, we can learn to gauge our atmospheric condition—the climate of our being—in any given situation. This tool is invaluable in reading where we are with the energy of the moment. With it we're able to tune in firsthand to the sane and confused aspects of any of the five energy families. With training we become sensitive to when we are "open" or "closed" to the moment. We can feel the moments when we open and when we close to energy, when we shine and when we are stuck. The more we practice recognizing this, the more we can see when our habitual tendencies are driving us out of the present moment.

When we are open to our own energy, we experience ourselves as warm and clear. When we are closed to our energy, we feel confused and stuck. So whether we are open or closed in a given moment very much determines how we view ourselves and consequently the world. When we experience a sense of well-being—as when we're open—we go with the flow. At those moments we can hang out with friends and feel comfortable and at ease, or we can attend a business meeting and feel on top of things. When we feel constricted—as when we're closed—we feel afraid or awkward. Our defense systems are up, and we're unable to clearly receive the energy of the present moment. We panic, our thoughts jumble up, and nothing we do goes very well.

I recently visited a castle in southern Switzerland. I love castles and am not usually afraid of heights, but as I stood on top of the tower, the wind suddenly began to gust. At the same time there was a glare from the sun that distorted my vision. I began to feel disoriented, groundless, and afraid. A cold chill went up my back as I looked over the edge of the wall, which had no railing, and saw the ground three hundred feet below. I had flashes of falling. I began talking to myself for reassurance: "The ground is beneath me. I'm stepping forward. Ahead is a railing. I'm reaching for the railing." The fear wasn't particularly necessary for my survival. In giving in to it, I closed down. As a result, I missed the present moment: the delight of the gusting wind, the light playing tricks with my eyes, the exhilarating feeling of height.

Our neurosis (closed) and our wisdom (open) exist in a common matrix of energy, as if they were alternating currents or the flip side of each other. Neither is solid or static. At times I get down on myself because of my quick reactivity toward people and events (karma energy). It puts people on edge with me. Yet that same energy saved my mother's life. When our car turned over in a ditch full of water, her arm was trapped under the seat back. While Dad and our dog exited through the window, I pulled her out, breaking her arm, but saving her life.

When we realize how insubstantial and fluid our energy is, we can learn to work with it on a deep level. We can tap into the power to transform confusion into wisdom. When we stay on the surface, it's a dualistic world: us and them, me and my enemy, sweet Sue and her crazy boyfriend. But when we open to the energetic depth of the moment and remain with it as it is, dualistic thinking falls away and we experience the full display of energy. In doing that, we also transcend the struggle between closed (confused) and open (sane).

Here are snapshots of our five main characters—vajra, ratna, padma, karma, and buddha—manifesting in both open and closed ways. Vajra Robert is extremely clear and can make simple statements that relax everyone in the midst of confusion (open). However, when his own confusion becomes overwhelming, he's likely to lash out at others with a cutting sharpness (closed). Ratna Geraldine is outwardly generous; there is a sense of comfort in her presence (open). But at times she can feel extremely needy and completely inadequate (closed). Padma Marita is a delightful, sensitive person to most of her friends (open), but when her primary relationship is not going well, she loses all sense of well-being and enjoyment (closed). Karma Luke is full of energy and accomplishes an amazing number of worthwhile activities (open), but if he feels anyone is trying to compete with him or block his energy, he exerts tremendous control to hold on to his territory (closed). Buddha Eric is a very accepting and spacious person (open), but when he feels overwhelmed, he becomes stuck and paralyzed. He just doesn't want to do anything (closed).

These examples illustrate how we teeter on the edge between our neurosis and our sanity. Whether we feel wise and peaceful or tense and irritable depends on our psychophysical barometer—how well we are tuned in to our own energy and that of the environment, as well as our willingness to work with it. What we learn in working with the energies is that the sane and neurotic tendencies are always there. They coexist, even within the same situation: Luke has a lot of energy and is driven by a need to control; Marita loves people and gets depressed when her relationship is not going well. We also learn that outer circumstances have the power to exacerbate the confusion: when Eric feels overwhelmed, he becomes stuck and paralyzed. We encounter an edge, and we shut down.

This neurotic shutdown is how we say, "Stop the world. I want to get off!" The point at which it is most likely to happen is when our expectations of how things "should" be are insulted by reality. Reality breaks through our filter of concepts, and it doesn't match the picture of how we think it should be. We feel frustrated and react emotionally. Because the situation doesn't meet our expectations, we resist what's happening by closing down in the style to which we've become accustomed. We can close down for an instant or for a lifetime.

When we use our psychophysical barometer to attune ourselves to energy, we give ourselves the gift of awareness. We can step beyond our mental gates to see and feel the energy of the moment. This liberates us into the possibility of changing our attitude. I once spent several weeks alone practicing meditation in a small cabin. During a storm one day, the wind was raging, and the rain came down in torrents. At moments I was afraid of being swept away. I thought my cabin might be torn from the hill and flung into the ocean. Then I felt irritated that the rain made so much noise pounding on the roof, that the wind rattled the windows so furiously. I also had moments of ease, when I could just enjoy the full magnificence of the storm's energy, without feeling fear or frustration. Finally I noticed that I was making up melodramas about the phenomena going on outside my cabin. I realized that a storm is simply a storm; it does not notice me or my reactions to it. Like all of nature, it simply is.

The same kind of reactivity creates all of our everyday melodramas. It is based not so much on what is happening as on our expectations. Perhaps your particular storm is your aggressive boss. You could react to her in several different ways, depending on how your two energies meet. You could cower in a corner feeling victimized or lash back at her feeling rebellious. Alternatively, you could relax into observing her display of energy and dance with it instead of reacting to it.

We can't ask a river to stop flowing. All we can do is make a bridge over it, swim in it, or watch the sunlight play on it, according to our appetite. We accept the river and appreciate it in our own way. Life is constantly challenging us to open to the situation at hand or shrink from it—to say yes or no to embracing the fullness of the moment. When we are open and welcoming, we experience the play of energies as spacious and full of possibility. When we freeze and withdraw from the world, we feel stuck, dense, and claustrophobic.

FREEZING ENERGY

There is a pattern to the process of freezing our energy. When we feel threatened—when a button gets pushed—we panic and immediately go into an ego alert. Ego is a pattern of defense mechanisms that we mistakenly tend to identify as (a) solid and (b) ourselves. In order for us to maintain the illusion of this solid identity of a self—which furthermore gives us the illusion of security—ego needs to feel in control. To do this, it is willing to shut down any sense of flexibility toward what we perceive as beyond our defensive wall. So our psychophysical barometer shuts down.

I personally experience the process of freezing into a solidified sense of self most blatantly in drastic events like upheavals at work or a rough patch in a relationship. The uncertainty becomes too threatening to bear, and I want to fill the void. There are various ways to do this—through analyzing, worrying, overworking, drinking, spacing out in front of the TV, overeating. Taking refuge in another identity to boost our sense of solidity ("Even though he left me, I have a job; therefore, I'm successful," or "I may have lost my job, but I still have a lover; therefore, I'm lovable") is another popular way to shut down. Whatever habitual coping mechanisms we use to do this, it's quite likely that we're blind to them. When we're unaware of how we constrict our energy, we perpetuate our own entrapment.

Whether we're talking about shutting down in the face of a crisis or the chronic numbing habits that shield us from everyday life, each of us tends to close off in a consistent way, following a progression of steps. First, we feel a sense of panic. We are threatened by the unknown, the unacceptable. Then we freeze: we can sense this on a physical level. Then a sequence of responses to that first freeze begins to unfold. We feel out what is happening and quickly move to a solidified view of what is going on.

Sometimes these responses happen gradually; sometimes they

take place so quickly that they may feel simultaneous. However, when we look closely, we may notice that they are actually sequential. When we pay attention to this sequence of responses, we begin to see how we become constricted, how we develop certain habits and patterns in an attempt to maintain a secure, safe self. We will notice that all our experiences have a reference point of "me." We create the fortification of "me," with credentials, house, car, hairstyle, manner of speaking, emotional tone, and so forth. The more threatening the world becomes, the more layers of "me" we put on, and the bigger "me" becomes.

CREATING OUR WORLD

Habits and patterns for coping often take the form of "story lines." We all develop scripts that filter the world for us and give us external verification. Let's accompany Jillian to a party and watch her script unfold. Jillian is in the best of moods, having fun, feeling relaxed and open. Glancing across the room, she sees a familiar man. Her free-flowing energy is interrupted, and she senses a sudden separation from her open self. At a subliminal level she notices how the man is dressed, his tone of voice, how he carries himself. She can't decide whether she's attracted to him, irritated by him, or indifferent. Finally she recognizes him as an old lover.

Jillian begins to edit the situation, her story line unfolds, and memory comes into play. She knits the past, present, and possible future into a fabric, imagining that she is being reunited with the love of her life after a prolonged and unjust separation. Her mind spins faster, filling in any gaps. Her story feels convincing and real. Jillian is no longer in an open, dancing space. She has become obsessed with a world of her own creation, inhabited only by herself and her version of this man. Jillian's projections have created a fantasy world, preventing her from participating in the creative flow in and around her.

We also create story lines when bad news prompts us to shore up a sense of self. One evening several summers ago during my monthly breast exam, I discovered several lumps. I froze. My mind went into high gear. My mother had cancer, I thought, so I must have cancer, too. I would need surgery and a lot of care. Who would take care of me? My cousin the doctor would know what to do. My mother died of cancer, so I would, too. What would my children do? They would struggle without their mother. My husband would have a hard time trying to raise the children alone. Within moments I had created a full-blown tragedy. When a visit to the doctor the next morning alleviated my fears, the story line lost its hold.

We create dramas like this all the time by clinging to expectations and assumptions about how we are and how the world is. We each direct and star in our own play, in which everyone has a defined role. We create this play to confirm our very existence. We play god, creating the world in our own image. When another person or the world at large presents a different version of reality, we're shocked at the alteration to our script. "How dare he treat me like that when I'm in love with him?" We're unaware that we have manufactured our worldview. We feel overwhelmed by the demands of a world that won't conform to our story, people who refuse to play their roles. We long to find some safe and manageable place.

REALMS: NEUROTIC VERSIONS OF REALITY

As we will see in the chapters on the individual buddha families, each is associated with a confused version of reality called a realm. A realm is what results from our interpretation of events and circumstances as seen through the filter of thoughts and emotions. We all create realms very much the way Jillian created her desire realm based on passion. We could create a hell realm full of aggression. Or we could create a jealous realm in which we dominate with control and manipulation. We are capable of experiencing all the realms, but as with the families, we each have our personal specialties. It depends on our style.

Here are nutshell descriptions of the six realms, the neurotic aspects of the families (buddha has two), using their traditional Buddhist names:

- If you live in perpetual anger, withdrawn and frozen in self-hatred or lashing out at others, you are in a *cold or hot hell realm* (vajra).
- If you feel needy, with a "poor me" attitude, you are in the *hungry ghost realm* (ratna).
- If you are filled with desire and perpetually manipulate situations to get what you want, you are in the *human realm* (padma).
- If you are continually on edge, wary of anyone who might get ahead of you, you are in the *jealous god realm* (karma).
- If you relate only to what is under your nose and ignore all else, you are in the *animal realm* (buddha). If you live in blissful ignorance, you are in the *god realm* (also buddha).

We create our version of the world by projecting our particular reaction to what is happening and then solidifying it into a realm. For example, if you are an angry person, everyone is a potential enemy; if you are a jealous person, everyone is in competition with you; if you are a passionate person, everyone is a friend, a lover. Our version becomes so solid that we are convinced by it, forgetting that it's our creation. Ironically the version of reality we create can, in turn, seem threatening to us, so we defend ourselves against it by taking an emotional stance. I caught myself doing this one evening when I came home late and projected on my husband that he was angry about it. I walked through the door angry and defensive, poised to justify my actions, to explain that what I had been doing was really important. I created my picture of the situation as well as my emotional defense. Likewise, in the story above, Jillian created her world—projected a reality—and then fell in love with her projected object. My husband had no such story line, and neither did Jillian's former lover.

Realms are our response to external circumstances. As children, we make our own choices about what we do when we want to avoid what is happening—hide in the animal realm, find religion and bliss out in the god realm, and so forth. Sometimes whole societies or cultures perpetuate a realm. Nepal is an example of a hungry ghost realm: on the one hand, there is utter poverty, and on the other hand, the rich get richer. Living there for a year, I felt a perpetual neediness in myself. It was not that I was in a state of poverty; rather, that was how the poverty around me affected me.

We can cycle through all the realms in a day or a lifetime. For example, Tania's great-grandmother experienced significantly different periods in her life, each of which could be seen as a realm. She was born into the god realm as part of the elite Russian aristocracy of Leningrad. Becoming bored with and critical of the elitist life and wanting to be more involved in the world, she became interested in politics. Although she knew she would be disowned by her family, she married a controversial politician anyway, hoping for political power for herself. This is the jealous god realm. Then she entered the human realm for a period, exemplified by a balance between material comfort, meaningful politics, the freedom to make choices in her life, and exploring her religious inclinations. She gave birth to three children.

However, her husband was revealed as a traitor, and their ideal world began to dissolve. With less money and fewer friends, she spent her days as a housewife trying to educate her children. She descended to the animal realm, just trying to survive. Then they were exiled to Poland, where they had nothing. Unable to get work or help, they were forced to beg for food. This is the hungry ghost realm.

Knowing full well that the government had exiled them to Poland as a fate worse than execution due to the Poles' extreme hatred toward Russians, her sense of fear and anger increased. She entered the hell realm. Her husband escaped Poland to Russia, only to be killed. She learned that her whole family had been extinguished during the revolution. She was in utter poverty with no one to help her or her children. The Poles spit on her, beat her, and made degrading comments about Russians. She began to lose touch with reality. One day, in an act of desperation, she tried to kill her children by tying them in burlap bags and drowning them in the river. Her oldest son, aged eight, freed himself and managed to convince his mother that he would help.

Something clicked, and she realized she must try to make it. Now she returned from the hell realm to the hungry ghost realm, with her son taking charge. He begged for food; made friends with a family of butchers, who gave them meat once a month; and got bread and potatoes from a compassionate farmer's wife. Able to care for her children again, she was back in the animal realm, surviving day by day.

Soon she was able to make a home, educate her children, and bring some integrity back into their lives. She was in the human realm again. Being in the human realm reminded her of what she once was and all the possibilities the world had to offer. She turned to religion. At the same time she began to want a better life. She spent less time with her children and more time outside the house seeking "a way out." She was in the jealous god realm. But then she contracted tuberculosis and suffered hallucinations and delusions. She became unaware of her surroundings, singing hymns. She no longer wanted to eat or drink. She was in the god realm, a blissful, fabricated world, where she died.

Whatever realm we find ourselves in, we use its strategies to ward off the world and make ourselves feel safe. We may feel safe for a while, but eventually the realm begins to seem like a prison. Like the people in Plato's cave who see only the shadows of other people passing, our view of life is narrow. We are constantly scheming with ourselves about how trusting or how protected we need to be in a given situation: "I'm not going to say hello to that person. I don't like her" (human realm). "I can't go along with this. It's against my principles" (hell realm). We spend a tremendous amount of energy maintaining our defensive boundaries. Being in a realm is like being in the ocean and, instead of enjoying the waves, struggling frantically to stay dry.

HOW WE THAW

Although it might seem discouraging to think of our life as a frozen, narrow, habitual pattern, the good news is that we are all capable of letting go of our fear-driven defenses and opening to what is. Every human being feels at least moments of openness. With practice those moments can become more frequent.

We start to thaw our fear simply by recognizing our stuckness. Then we make friends with our numbing habits. For example, for years jealousy was my habitual response to many situations. When I became aware of my jealousy and curious about it, I realized that at its kernel was an appreciation for the person of whom I was jealous. Seeing that, I began to practice going beyond the closed-off jealous feeling into the open place where I felt appreciation. Opening came from going deeper into the place where I was stuck. That very stuckness held all the potential for moving forward. But I was unable to use its energy until I had embraced what I wanted to deny. In wanting to push the habitual jealous reaction away, I was rejecting a precious part of myself. In accepting myself, including the habitual jealousy, I discovered the wisdom in the neurosis. Welcoming pain or unwanted feelings without making judgments about them is how we begin to transform confusion into wisdom.

EXERCISE: BECOMING A PSYCHOPHYSICAL BAROMETER

This exercise is about cultivating your ability to be a psychophysical barometer. Make a commitment to be aware, as you go through your day, of when you are open and when you are closed. A simple way to determine whether you are open or closed is to tune in to your breathing. When we are closed, we tend to hold our breath. As some wise person said, "Fear is just excitement without the breath." When we are open, we breathe more easily. Sanity comes from a sense of being synchronized within ourselves. It's breathing easy, going with the flow, riding the wave. We feel pleasure and a lightness of being. Use your breath as a reference point. You can do this one day at a time. When you get up in the morning, resolve to be sensitive to open and closed energy. Over time you will find that you can do this automatically, all the time.

EXERCISE: RECOGNIZING HOW YOU GO INTO A REALM

Once you have some experience in recognizing whether you are open or closed, you can begin to explore how the closing-off process works for you. Here are some questions to stimulate your exploration:

- What triggers the freeze, the split? What is your experience of the panic? How do you close off from the world?
- What does the uncertainty feel like? What are your body sensations? How is your intuitive intelligence feeling out the situation?
- What do you perceive is happening? What is your impulsive reaction? What are the subtle feelings of attraction, revulsion, or indifference?
- How do you name what is happening? How do you interpret, categorize, and form an opinion? What kinds of thoughts and emotions are being generated?
- How do you maintain your intuitive feelings, your impulsive reactions, and your opinions and emotions? What is your mental chatter saying that weaves together your story line and justifications? At what point does the story line feel solid? What realm are you in?

WORKING WITH THE FIVE ENERGIES

The following five chapters contain detailed descriptions of the five energies in both their wisdom and neurotic possibilities. We will discuss how each energy manifests its sanity, clarity, and brilliance as well as how it manifests its confusion, neurosis, and stuckness. We will see how this is displayed in our inner world of thoughts and emotions as well as in the outer world of our physical environment. We will see how we can transform our relationship to the five energies by changing our attitude.

Each chapter ends with some suggested activities that you can use to deepen your experience of that particular energy quality. These activities will enhance your sense of the five energies. I suggest focusing on each energy, one at a time, for a week or more.

4

Vajra: Clarity

WISDOM ASPECT, SANE POSSIBILITIES

In its open, brilliant, and pure state, vajra energy is crystal clarity. It is associated with the color blue, the element water, and the sense of sight. Vajra energy reflects its surroundings like a calm, clear pool of water, without distortion or bias. Thus vajra wisdom is mirrorlike: it sees things as they are.

The environment of vajra is a mountainous landscape where the air is cool and refined. Winter is its season. Picture a bright winter day, the air crisp and fresh. Sunlight on the snow dazzles the eye. The landscape is finely etched and full of all sorts of thought-provoking sharpnesses. The textures of objects and their relationships are clear and vivid. Ice-frozen branches catch the sun. Icicles add a jewel-like accent.

Vajra people's primary mode of operating is mental. They radiate a sense of "I know." They have a passion to know, to understand, to learn. They dwell in a refined world in which the mind can open to its own intelligence. Their minds are sharp, like the freshness of a winter dawn. Their learning style is intellectual, analytical, and principled. They take a big view. Vajras can be accomplished scholars. They dwell on mountain peaks and in ivory towers or nowadays more probably in front of their computers. They are always searching for something interesting to know. At best their knowing arises from the present moment and is relevant to the immediacy of the situation. And once they know, they want to explain.

For the vajra type there are two ways of knowing: panoramic and detailed. On the one hand, vajras are interested in a visionary overview. They always want to see a map of the terrain before they proceed. In any situation they relate first to the general ideas and basic principles, in order to become aware of all the possibilities. Hidden corners or unexplored areas are anathema to them. Their intellect must illuminate everything from all directions.

Also, vajra people have a passion for detail, precision, and clarity. They are thorough, methodical, and systematic. They like to see how details fit into an overall structure. The more viewpoints they have, the more prepared they feel. They develop strategies to counteract problems and then strategies to counteract the strategies. Because people with a preponderance of vajra energy are so mental and forward-looking, the forehead and chest are the areas of the body where their energy focuses.

Vajra people think and speak either in simple, clear statements or in complex, elegantly constructed arguments. In either case they follow a train of thought point by point. Their speech is crisp and precise, with no superfluity. Mentally they tend to be conceptual; they relate well with abstract principles. They want to know the logical relation of one thing to another. They see the world in terms of patterns: maps, guides, principles, logic. They want to know the where, why, and what of things. "What's the setup here? What are the rules? How does it work?" They can be philosophical: "What is life? What is the essence?" In terms of their relationships with others, they want to know histories, worldviews, passions, strengths, and weaknesses.

The clear-minded quality of vajra people, with its accurate and brilliant reflection of what is, has a pacifying and calming effect on others. Not only are vajras able to see what's happening clearly and without bias, but they also have the ability to highlight a broader perspective. Even in complex situations, they can see the advantages and disadvantages of different positions, the challenges that moving in any particular direction might present. Since vajra people see both sides of an argument with clarity and without having to be right, they can help defuse struggle or conflict. There is an unyielding evenness about vajras that cuts the energy of emotional upheaval. They tend to be reasonable and dependable, unflustered by their own or others' emotions.

This calm, even quality is the epitome of the vajras' potential for sane action. People with a preponderance of this energy make great mediators, facilitators, and leaders. They can bring everyone around to a common ground so they can work together. They see through neurotic manipulation and stop it cold. When there is a maze of so-lidified hostility on both sides, they can cut through the fixed positions to find the points of agreement. They see chaos and conflict but do not exacerbate the discord by adding their own mental baggage to the situation. They clean up messes, create order, clarify the environment. They bring harmony by clearly seeing the obstacles to it. Other people are drawn to the vajras' astute judgment.

Vajra people are observers, seers. Their wisdom is tempered by a compassion that comes from seeing so clearly. Others turn to them for the final answer. They exude a dignified strength, a sense of being so definite that nothing can attack them. They are impenetrable, in-destructible, like a diamond. There is no room for chaos. They can be objective in a positive sense and not get caught up in emotional cloudiness or personal vendettas.

My friend Peter has a strong dose of vajra in his personality. When we attend meetings together, he sits there calmly as others make their points, become heated over the issues, and at times digress and lose their train of thought. At the end of the discussion, he speaks up, succinctly summarizing the main points. He points out the polarities in people's positions and presents a middle way that accommo-dates all views. This sense of perspective often allows everyone else to relax and agree on a course of action.

Vajras have a tremendous sense of integrity. They like the containment that boundaries provide. If the boundaries are sketchy, they will make them firm. This is how they create an orderly world that has structure and form. Imagine a formal party in a splendidly decorated room, in which elaborately dressed people are behaving with impeccable manners and decorum. This is a vajra world. To some, such a defined structure might look rigid or constricting, but in fact, the form itself makes a space in which elegance, grace, and clarity can arise.

Vajra people make good leaders, diplomats, scientists, surgeons, dentists, watchmakers, engineers, and computer programmers. In terms of a religion or spiritual path, the philosophical and intellectual aspects are what attract them. Their style of dress could be simple or elegant. They like solid, uncomplicated colors, which might be bright, with just the right ornamentation.

On an emotional level, vajra people have a sense of distance, reserve, and cool detachment. They might feel things deeply, but they don't express those feelings in obvious ways. They often feel more comfortable in platonic relationships than in romantic ones. They are inclined to be warm and gentle rather than hot and passionate. They enjoy playful verbal repartee that shows off their quick-tongued, cutting wit. They delight in dry and philosophical wordplay stemming from their ability to see all the angles. At their best, they are light, sparkling, and bubbly, like a fresh mountain spring.

A therapeutic approach that attracts vajras is psychoanalysis, with its intellectual understanding of emotional dynamics and how the mind works. They run the risk of becoming so involved in dissecting emotions and psychological dynamics that any insight becomes merely one more thing to analyze. They might appreciate shiatsu massage, which is clean and precise.

Cultures that have a well-defined vision and a strong sense of propriety and decorum belong to the vajra family. A good example is the Japanese affinity for visual order, precision, a highly refined sense of decorum, and collective principles overriding individual will. The

Scandinavian countries, Germany, German Switzerland, England, and to some extent the United States also have strong vajra qualities.

Vajra people's visual sense is very keen. They want to see how things line up and are connected. In visual art vajra space is sharply defined, with a geometrical design. Vajras prefer bright, bold, monochromatic colors with a smooth, almost metallic texture. Cubism, constructivism, and certain aspects of pointillism—seen in the work of such artists as Mondrian and Klee—display these qualities. M. C. Escher's work also has vajra qualities, particularly in its balance of playfulness and self-mockery. Vajra qualities are also evident in conceptual art and graphic art. Photography and filmmaking appeal to vajra people, who are always focusing the lens, framing the world, finding just the right composition. Japanese or modern architecture has vajra's clean-cut lines and sharply delineated spaces, with a sense of refinement. Architecture that uses light, mirrors, crystals, and stained glass also has vajra qualities, in that vajra spaces are generally sharp, uplifting, and light.

Vajra music is brilliant and clear, like the work of Mozart, Bach, and Edgar Varèse. The elemental vajra sound is an elongated *ee*, penetrating space.

Classical ballet, with its focus on refined physical lines and postures that go far beyond what seems natural, is a good example of vajra dance. Merce Cunningham is a contemporary choreographer who delights in working with vajra energy, particularly in his approach to time and space.

Literary forms that embody vajra sensibility are classical poetry such as English sonnets and Japanese haiku. Scientific journals and technical manuals belong to the vajra family. Journalism combines elements of vajra and karma.

Sports like skiing, fencing, karate, and Japanese archery (kyudo) have the one-pointedness and precision of vajra. Japanese samurai, who take vows binding themselves to higher principles and fight with total commitment, are the epitome of the vajra mind-set.

Vajra qualities manifest in diverse ways in terms of food and drink:

gin and tonics, the Japanese tea ceremony, and French nouvelle cuisine. It could be said that vajra animals do not make the best of pets. Eagles, sharks, and swordfish are better admired from a distance.

INTENSIFIED PATTERNS, NEUROTIC VIEW

When vajra energy becomes constricted, solidified, or closed, the desire to see things clearly becomes a neurotic compulsion. There is tremendous fear of being surprised, confused, or overwhelmed by irrational or chaotic circumstances. This can lead to a tense alertness and strong need for control, which is fed by denial of disturbing or confusing forces. Vajra people panic when they don't understand; answers are their security.

In its confused mode, the energy of the vajra mind spins out overlapping thoughts and ties itself into knots. Logic becomes convoluted. Overfed by intellectual constructs and analyses and an excessive attention to details, it makes things more complicated than necessary. The resulting perspective is overly mental. Because it does not arise from a direct perception of the situation, it loses its connection to what is happening. A compulsion to systematize takes over. Vajras knit everything into a tight conceptual framework so there is a nice, cogent intellectual answer for every question. (Think of people who never make a move without reading their horoscope, for example; conversely they are able to explain everything that happens to them by relating it to planetary movements.) Facts that don't fit are ignored or rationalized. Vajra energy that has intensified into a habitual pattern spins out ideas without regard for their relationship to reality. General rules are applied without seeing what is going on; specific rules are applied mechanically. Ultimately, in trying too hard to figure it all out, vajra people can become fuzzy in their thinking.

When they lose their open perspective, vajras become self-righteous and closed. Their "I know" becomes "I'm right." They manage to fit everything into their point of view to justify and confirm it. They listen to someone else's opinion only to establish their own more firmly. They never admit they are wrong. Their belief systems become rigid and tight. The arrogance of "I know it all" develops. When their energy is frozen, vajra people are ideological, opinionated, authoritarian, narrowly moralistic, dogmatic, and rigid. They are constantly asserting themselves. They enjoy conflict as a way of connecting with others and love to outsmart their opponents.

For vajras the greatest sense of inadequacy comes from feeling that they don't understand or see enough, combined with a need to be right or perfect. If they aren't perfect, they feel guilty and ashamed. They live in a world of "shoulds" and perpetually feel guilty. When their confidence breaks down, they react by establishing territory, warding off, rejecting, keeping things at a distance. Their coolness becomes a frozen facade, and they seem impenetrable, uptight, and detached. They deaden themselves with systems and concepts. Although on the surface their position might still seem reasonable, it is in fact stubborn and dogmatic.

Their concern for boundaries hardens into a protective stance. They turn inward, building walls around themselves so they can maintain their own version of the world. The irony is that in pushing away whatever doesn't fit into their perspective, they become cornered by their own aggression. Their walls make them feel alienated.

Because vajra people want a clear, orderly world, they fear emotionality—particularly passion—as unpredictable, confusing, and fundamentally incomprehensible. Because they fear being trapped by emotions, they simply don't feel; they suppress. Being emotionally alienated, they are awkward around others. Although they long for contact, they can't accept it.

Closed-off vajras need to convince the world that they hold the correct view, which leads to a chronic feeling of anger. They dislike the reality of the world and are perpetually resentful, which creates an environment of aggression. They either blame someone else or are hard on themselves—or more likely both. They can't escape the roles of attacker or victim. When rigidified, vajra's sharpness and clarity become criticism, harshness, and irritability. The clear water turns cloudy, churned up by defensiveness and aggression.

The vajra person's attention to form and etiquette can become another way of keeping the world at a distance. The intricate ways of doing things and well-defined mores involved with proper manners, as in Japanese and English cultures, can become an obsession. There is a strong notion of the right way and the wrong way of doing things. An extreme example is the Japanese tradition of hara-kiri. If a person failed in the performance of his duty as a warrior or servant of the state, the honorable solution was to commit suicide.

As far as health goes, vajras can get so caught up in their heads that they neglect their bodies. They may not even notice when they're hungry. They are prone to headaches and upper backaches or even a general stiffness and rigidity in their bodies. Their speediness and high reactivity make them ready to jump, pursue, and criticize. This combination of aggression and intellect creates an airtight atmosphere that can result in suicide.

When this energy is most intensified, vajra people live in a realm of sheer hell, a place of continuous oppression, irritation, and anger. At best they are perpetually sarcastic and cynical. At worst they live in either an alienated, frozen, rigid world or a reactive, caustic, combative world. Fear and aggression build up. They have a sense of torturing and being tortured. There is a fascination with being an oppressor, defeating others, lording it over them. The mirrorlike wisdom becomes a black hole of aggression with seemingly no way out.

TRANSFORMING NEUROSIS INTO SANITY

The process of transforming or transmuting neurosis into sanity is the ultimate challenge of working with the energies. The transformative power of this process lies in the deep understanding that fundamentally each energy is neutral; it is our attitude toward it that determines whether it is neurotic or sane. Each energy teeters on a razor's edge between sanity and confusion. The pith instruction is to ride the primary emotion of the particular family. Doing this will show us that on a primal level, neurosis and sanity are inseparable. Making friends with the essential nature of the emotion instead of trying to turn away from it or cover it up offers the possibility of liberating it. Although the story line and the quality of the basic energy may differ, the process remains the same. We will explore this process in greater depth in chapter 13.

The transformative power of vajra energy is particularly helpful to understand because it works with anger, which is so common an emotion for most of us. Change happens when we are able to see the intelligence in an aggressive outburst or an inner-directed anger like stonewalling. It is the ability to see how someone is actually making sense though he or she is full of rage.

As we have seen, vajra's basic nature is clarity. However, people all too often express their clarity by becoming angry. There is an intelligence and a clarity in the anger, which, when not solidified, can inform. When it becomes too solidified, most people want to either blame (hot anger) or leave (cold anger). When people are willing to stay with the anger and let it thaw, it becomes the wisdom of clarity.

For example, when Michael offers his clarity to his business colleagues without an ax to grind, his clarity can illuminate difficult situations. It cuts through confusion and emotional biases by simply reflecting things as they are. "There's no problem; let's look at it this way." This has the quality of pacifying situations. Vajra people vacillate between simply being clear and trying to impose their clarity on others with a sharp, aggressive edge.

A working group came to a point at which anger emerged as sharp criticism of one another, the situation, and the group leader. At first this development caused confusion and a sense that the working relationship was no longer tenable. However, the leader, experienced in working with the five energies, was pleased that previously unspoken issues were being brought out. She appreciated that the clarity—albeit embedded in anger—was shining through. She saw that the members of the group needed to recognize their intelligence in the situation. What happened was that the various issues evolved into work points. In addition, when the group's direction became more clear, some people simply did not feel aligned with it and chose to leave. For those who remained, the situation proved to be both empowering and binding, as their expression and intelligence were given free rein. This could not have happened if the energy of anger had been repressed.

VAJRA ACTIVITIES

To have an experiential sense of the quality of the vajra family, choose from the following suggested activities. You can also turn to appendix A, "The Five Wisdom Energies at a Glance," to familiarize yourself with further aspects of the family. If something grabs your interest, develop your own activity around it—like paying attention to the movement element or body part.

There is no "right" way to do these activities. Everyone will have his or her unique experience of the energy. Tuning in to the qualities of a particular family might feel familiar, like coming home; or foreign, like visiting a new place; or you might have a strong negative reaction to the quality: you just don't want to go there. The point is to notice how doing these activities—or just thinking about them— affects your experience of yourself.

Focus on vajra energy for a week or more.

- Wear clothes with simple lines, solid colors, or geometric patterns, and ornamentation with clean-cut lines.
- Create order in your living or work space. Be very specific about where you put things and delineate the spaces between things. Set aside an area, such as a small table, to create a display of objects with vajra qualities.
- Notice places, situations, and people that embody vajra energy.
- Be very conscious of looking at things, near and distant: the de-

tails of a flower or snowflake, the moon and stars on a clear night, a photography exhibit, the paintings in an art gallery.

- Take photographs and look for striking contrasts between light and shade. Look at familiar objects through both ends of a pair of binoculars. Look at mirrors and see how they play with space and light.
- Make a drawing using only straight lines.
- Pick up on speech idioms in yourself and others, such as "It's very clear," "I don't quite understand," "It's confusing," "Explain it to me," "What is the basic principle?" "I should," "I feel guilty."
- Play music in which you find the following qualities: brilliant, clear, clean, light. Listen to pieces with very precise or staccato rhythms that use instruments like the flute, violin, or bells.
- Choose something you have always wanted to learn. Go to the library or a Web site and research the subject. Think about it, paying attention to the overview and the details. Share your understanding with someone.
- Take note of amusing ideas that come to mind that reflect vajra energy.
- Envision your life in the future. Where would you like your life to be in three or five years' time?

5

Ratna: Enrichment

WISDOM ASPECT, SANE POSSIBILITIES

Ratna's wisdom is equanimity; it needs nothing. The world is sufficient—abundant and plentiful. A golden yellow color that radiates richness characterizes ratna energy. Its element is earth. At its best, ratna energy is deeply settled, full, and satisfied.

Ratna people feel expansive, complete, and fulfilled. Like the sun shining without discrimination, ratnas appreciate the importance and worth of all things. They see everyone as equal, sharing a common humanity. They view positive and negative experiences as equally rich.

Ratnas are fundamentally hospitable and generous. They include, accommodate, embrace, and offer. They bring richness out in others. They are infinitely resourceful, full of new opportunities and possibilities. They can make the most of any situation. Their passion is to encompass the whole, taking it in and exulting in it. They want dominion over the world. They are "bigger than life."

Ratna energy contains a sense of fertility and potentiality, like being pregnant. The earth does not discriminate what grows on it but accepts and nourishes all. Ratnas feel anchored to the earth with a grounded physicality. They have keen senses of smell and taste.

They orient to the world in a tactile way; they want to be in touch with everything. They are sensual people.

The ratna environment is lush, like a tropical rain forest where the air is warm and moist and smells of living things. Rotting matter provides fertile ground for new growth. Flowers bloom abundantly, and fruit ripens and falls. Autumn, the time of harvest and celebration, with an abundance of wholesome foods and a focus on home and family, most typifies ratna energy. Ratnas love Thanksgiving. They are also in their element in the late afternoon of Christmas Day, surrounded by decorations and piles of opened presents, sitting around the fire in cozy, overstuffed furniture, joking and laughing and listening to someone tell a long story.

Ratna people have a confident, authentic pride. They emit a sense of dignity and exhibit a regal bearing, like kings and queens holding court on jeweled thrones. They might like to wear vibrant clothes and lots of ornamentation. They can also express their abundance more simply, like the earthy farmer with strong ties to his land, animals, and family; the great cook who provides feasts for everyone; or the mother who nurtures whomever she touches.

The ornately elaborate art of the baroque period most captures ratna energy, as does the opulence found in the cultures of the Ottoman Empire, old Russia, and the Ming dynasty of China. The European Renaissance had this sense of abundance, and certain painters from that period—like Brueghel and Rubens—exhibit ratna energy. The Catholic Church and Tibetan Buddhism have strong ratna qualities. American consumerism and the art events of the 1960s called happenings, with their anything-goes attitude, also display this quality. Ratna energy is exemplified by massive, solid, or elaborate architecture. Medieval and baroque castles, as well as art deco, typify this style.

Ritual dance, replete with meaning and symbolism and objects to entice the senses, as well as some forms of court dance and coronations, are very ratna. African dance, belly dance, and the contemporary form called contact improvisation have ratna qualities. They are often characterized by a rooted stance and steady, slow, confident movements, with full, expansive gestures and an upright back. The arms and chest tend to be open, the fingers spread. The dance often includes circular, rounded gestures, encompassing the whole space.

Music on a grand scale, such as operas or large choral works, embodies ratna energy. Composers such as Wagner, Beethoven, Brahms, and Tchaikovsky evoke the ratna sense of profound emotion and drama. The elemental sound of ratna is an *ooh,* felt deep in the belly.

We find ratna energy in emotional, epic novels with complicated, elaborate plots and many characters. The books of Tolstoy, Dostoyevsky, Dickens, and Gabriel García Márquez display these qualities.

Ratna people learn by amassing and retaining large amounts of information. Their thinking is thorough and elaborate. They can give comprehensive, elaborate explanations of the smallest of subjects and provide descriptions rich in detail. They may have huge libraries from which they draw desired information. They surf the Internet for more and more things to know.

Ratnas like their spirituality to be emotional, devotional, and fervent. They require that their religion provide a sense of intensity. They connect with the passion of prayer. In terms of therapy, ratna people might seek a body-centered therapy, because of their sensuality, or one that focuses on emotions or deals with family issues, like reparenting. Environmental therapy, which highlights the importance of nurturing and support, also has this quality.

Rich, sumptuous foods such as eggnog and meat with gravy feed ratna energy. Animals with a ratna quality are either flashy and bold, like tropical birds, or large and heavy, like elephants, whales, bears, and pigs.

INTENSIFIED PATTERNS, NEUROTIC VIEW

When ratna energy is exaggerated, it becomes prideful and arrogant. Neurotic ratnas are self-important, puffed up, and grandiose, saying,

"I am substantial, resourceful, and have what it takes." Ratna people are ostentatious; they tend to take over a space to such an extent that others feel suffocated and oppressed. They need to confirm themselves and shore up their self-importance by making a large impact on the world. When things fall apart, they prop themselves up with pride. They want to be at the center of the world and the principal object of attention. They tend to talk loudly and incessantly.

When ratna people lose their sense of fullness and richness, they sink into a poverty mentality marked by perpetual neediness—the hungry ghost realm. They absorb what is around them like a sponge, then feed on it. They are like a bottomless pit. They see the wealth and variety of the world as outside them, beyond reach. Their inner world feels paltry. "I'm not good enough; I don't count," they think. They feel small and helpless in a big world.

Closed off by this sense of poverty, ratnas can be very greedy. They want to consume, and they can never get enough. Something is always missing. In Tibetan Buddhism a hungry ghost is pictured as a being with a large belly and a small neck—a big appetite and no way to fill it. Ratnas can't enjoy what they have because they're always looking for more, always thinking the best is "out there." Desiring and then consuming is ratnas' idea of satisfaction. Neurotic ratnas alternate between obsessive grasping and consuming, and giving up hope of ever having enough and wallowing in self-pity.

Ratna people are continually concerned with how much they have, how much they're worth. Expansion feels good; contraction feels painful. They are possessive and territorial. They take from others and hold on tight to what they have—like the godfather who protects his family but will kill to get what he wants. They collect indiscriminately—knowledge, food, pleasure, friends, property, information, spiritual experiences, memories, psychological gratification, and love. They are conspicuous consumers. Everything they touch becomes a possession, a confirmation of their existence.

Ratnas fiercely protect what they have accumulated. They become stingy, paranoid about things being stolen. Their possessions become a burden. They heedlessly indulge and accumulate, and then begin to suffocate, drowning in their lake of butter and honey. Impoverishment leads to expansiveness, which leads to claustrophobia.

In work relationships ratnas lord it over others. They are overbearing and oppressive. In personal relationships they are grasping and suffocating. They are overly demonstrative and inconsiderate, and they are generous to a fault. They gush and carry on. Ratna mothers are possessive; they nurture and devour. Male ratnas are often boorish, sloppy, and backslapping. Mud wrestling could be the quintessential ratna sport. Ratna lovers are lush, tending toward the disgusting. Separation is intensely painful for them.

Ratna people can be emotionally exaggerated and intense. When they lose confidence in their resourcefulness, they become helpless and feed off others' energy. They constantly seek reassurance, affection, and approval. The combination of neediness and pride can create a perpetual drama of hurt feelings and emotional outbursts. Too proud to give in, they hold grudges.

Neurotic ratnas can be skinny or fat. Their health issues center around eating disorders—anorexia and bulimia—and addictions. The consuming diseases of cancer and candida exemplify ratna energy. The drained and helpless feeling of chronic fatigue has a ratna quality.

TRANSFORMING NEUROSIS INTO SANITY

As we saw in chapter 4 ("Vajra: Clarity"), the process of transmuting neurosis into sanity is the ultimate challenge in terms of working with the energies. Please refer to page 40 in that chapter for a brief explanation or wait until chapter 13 for a fuller one.

The basic nature of ratna is richness. Ratnas vacillate between experiencing and taking pride in their own richness and feeling inadequate and inferior because they sense that the richness is outside of them, beyond their grasp. At times they feel a tremendous hunger and are needy and greedy for both possessions and attention. They crave more and more, overindulge, and yet never get enough. At other times they are full of pride, boasting about what they have.

Martha lives alone in a home that she decorated in a rich, lavish style, full of interesting objects and plants and collections of this and that from her travels abroad. She takes great pride in her house, even guiding tours through it periodically. She has many friends and loves keeping in touch with them. However, when she has some time on her hands, she feels an intense sense of worthlessness and tends to overeat to fill the void. She is quite overweight.

It takes Martha many years to become aware of this pattern in herself: her sense of well-being and pride when her life is full of things, people, and events, contrasted with her sense of emptiness when it is not. Working with the pattern of overeating has never helped. It feels harsh and critical to diet. However, with the help of a therapist, she begins to learn to catch those moments when she wants to eat—those devastatingly empty moments when the world feels like a wasteland—and then stay with that feeling. Acknowledging her fear, Martha enters the very energy she most dreads. She becomes curious about it. She sees that the energy does not necessarily have to be overwhelming. It is just her energy. She can stay with it, make friends with it. When she lets herself just be with the empty energy without trying to cover it up, she experiences her inner richness as it is, with neither poverty nor pride. She no longer needs to fill her emptiness with food because she does not feel separate from the world of abundance.

RATNA ACTIVITIES

To have an experiential sense of the quality of the ratna family, choose from the following suggested activities. Appendix A, "The Five Wisdom Energies at a Glance," might give further ideas for developing your own activity—like coloring or painting using ratna qualities. Remember that the basic point is to notice how doing these activities—or just thinking about them—affects your experience of yourself.

Focus on ratna energy for a week or more.

* Dress elaborately, choosing fabrics with appealing textures and rich colors. Wear lots of jewelry and scarves or a colorful tie.
* Bring a greater sense of richness into your home and workplace by adding more plants, fabrics, and lamps or indirect lighting.
* Go to places where there is richness of sights, smells, tastes, and touch: a garden or flower shop, a farmers' market, a museum, a fabric store, a jewelry shop, a pastry shop, a magazine shop, or a store selling body oils, soaps, and scents.
* Invite some friends over for dinner or a party. Be generous in preparing food, drink, and decorations.
* Start a collection of postcards, stamps, photographs, or whatever attracts you.
* Work in your garden or with your houseplants. Enjoy the feel of the earth and the smells of the flowers.
* Get a massage with scented oil.
* Pick up on speech idioms in yourself and others that use the superlative or in general reflect a sense of exaggeration or drama.
* Play music in which you find the following qualities: regal, grand, expansive, and full. Seek out choral or operatic works. Try Beethoven, Wagner, Tchaikovsky, and Brahms.
* Take note of amusing ideas that come to mind that reflect ratna energy.
* Enjoy indulging yourself.

6

Padma: Passion

At its best padma energy opens to the immediacy and preciousness of each moment. Padma people want to have strong contact with what is attractive and feel it fully. They delight in intimate connections. They want to become one with the world. They want things to be fiery hot, intensely red. Padma people have a keen sensitivity to the ambient tone of things and the dynamics between people. They are able to dissolve the boundary between themselves and others. They are full of life.

The wisdom energy of this family can be extremely attractive to other people. Padmas exhibit a wholesome goodness. They have confidence in their own lovability, with no need of outside confirmation. They are capable of great compassion, empathy, warmth, and love. They are accommodating and easygoing, with a childlike innocence that delights in everything. Padma people are so touched by the vitality of the world that their hearts break; they live wide open. Because their awareness is discriminating, padmas are selective in their choices; they appreciate beauty and cultivate refined tastes.

Padma is the energy of falling in love, with all its bittersweet quality. Padma love is perpetually unrequited, because a padma can never fully possess the object of desire. Embracing the pleasure and pain of love has a poignant, heart-piercing quality. The shape for this family is a half circle; padma feels that it never can be quite whole. The Japanese have a word for this feeling—*aware* (ah-WA-ray), meaning sad beauty, a sweetness tinged with sorrow.

Padmas know with their hearts. They rely on intuition rather than intellect. They have hunches, feelings about things. Their minds are flexible, and they have the ability to let go of thoughts. Their thinking is fluid, not logical in a linear way, so they can shift gears and make leaps in logic with impulsive daring. Padmas perceive without bias, because they see the essence and fullness of everything. Sensing the big picture, they can wander without getting lost.

With their intimate sensibility, padmas describe the world in a specific, concrete, and sense-oriented way. They tell stories using innuendo, imagery, analogy, and metaphor. Dreams and symbolism are important to them, and they appreciate fairy tales. In combining with other energies, the padma family is most versatile because of its fluid, chameleon-like quality. Padmas learn in a personal, even idiosyncratic way, through imagery and creative expression.

The parts of the body associated with padma energy include the neck, throat, eyes, and hands—communication centers. In the heat of passion, erogenous zones fill with padma energy. The sense perception associated with padma is hearing. Padmas listen deeply, with great compassion. They speak from the heart. They draw out other people and engage them with their easygoing, pleasant manner and gentle voice. This sense of pleasure and promise magnetizes others.

Because they dissolve boundaries, padmas make genuine contact with others. They constantly seek relationship, tuning in to and merging with another, reaching the most intimate places and uncovering what is hidden. They have a special ability to penetrate to the heart in an intuitive way. In a love relationship, they require balanced partnerships of genuine communication. They want both merging and individuality, closeness and spaciousness.

Padmas are willing to be present, whether what is happening is positive or negative. They provide spontaneous hospitality. At their most outgoing, padma people are radiantly charismatic and appreciative, exuberant and witty. They sap the strength from any resistance to their presence. Their intrinsic beauty creates energy. Padmas feel the world is endlessly hospitable to them, and they always seem to get what they want. They inspire others to laughter or tears. Being around a padma person makes you love yourself.

Padma people can be highly visible, outrageous, and appealing, like Scarlett O'Hara, Mick Jagger, Marilyn Monroe, and Princess Diana. Although they often wear flashy, colorful clothes, with lots of ornamentation, they maintain a sense of civility, elegance, and refinement, a charm with muted intensity. The Japanese word that captures this energy is *iki,* which in the geisha culture refers to a refined sophistication with a touch of sexual allure, like a formal hairdo with one wisp of hair falling down. Another padma image is that of an ingenue, a young woman who is delightfully innocent yet aware of her charm.

Padmas are playful, flirtatious, and seductive. They like to socialize. They enjoy noncompetitive group sports and party or theater games. Sitting in a café discussing the intricacies of life and art or hanging out in a bar meeting and flirting with a string of people are padma activities. The world of high fashion, the glitzy seductiveness of Madison Avenue, and the entertainment world have profited handsomely from people's attraction to padma energy.

Padma people like warm climates in which the orientation is toward camaraderie and sensual pleasure. Padmas want to touch, make contact, bathe in perfumed water, have a massage. Their world is charged with sexuality and exoticism. Strong padma elements exist in cultures of southern Europe: on the Mediterranean, in southern France and Italy, as well as in the South Seas, Bali, California, and Hawaii. The padma landscape is gardens, flowering meadows, and rolling hills. Padma energy is most prevalent at sunset, the bewitching twilight hour, and is captured by a garden party, with soft music, pastel shades, and delicate food, as well as by spring, with its balmy days, flowers bursting into bloom, and people emerging from their houses to enjoy the warmth.

The padma family is the realm of the visual artist, full of sensual, creative energy. The impressionist and romantic periods, with their emphasis on color and light rather than line and volume, characterize this family. The work of Monet, Rodin, Renoir, Toulouse-Lautrec, and Degas evoke the padma sensibility of intimacy and pleasure.

The way padmas connect to a religious path is with their hearts. They feel strong personal devotion to religious figures. As spiritual leaders, padma people make close connections with their followers. Others who manifest padma energy include glamorous performers, therapists, and babies.

For therapy padma people seek styles that are very immediate and emotionally engaging. Process-oriented group therapy in which personal interactions occur in the moment best satisfy this family. Gestalt therapy's work with inner dialogue among parts of oneself would make sense to padmas, as would transactional analysis, a more emotional approach to psychoanalysis. The body therapy most exemplifying this family would be sensual massage. Padmas also love art therapy, being able to express themselves without conceptual overlay.

Padma music can be poignant and sad or playful, romantic, and lyrical. The works of Debussy, Schubert, and Chopin capture padma energy, as do the blues and romantic love songs. Padma energy is defined by peak moments. The primal sound for this energy is *e* (eh), which internally massages the throat area, the center of communication.

Padma dance is expressionistic, ranging from the pas de deux of ballet to ballroom dancing, belly dancing, and striptease. It tends to be undulating, sensuous, and ever-changing, with indirect circular movements. Padma movement could also be full of suspension and hovering, joining and leaving.

Padma literature includes poetry, novels, and the lyrics of love songs. Magazines are designed to play up this energy; they magnetize and entertain us in doctors' offices and airplanes when we want to be seduced into someplace other than where we are.

Padma environments and architecture are pleasure-oriented, with soft, concave, receptive spaces, attention to color, and a warm, inviting quality. Padma food is flavorful and beautifully presented, like nouvelle cuisine or hors d'oeuvres. Padmas love pets, particularly baby animals, with whom they can cultivate close relationships.

INTENSIFIED PATTERNS, NEUROTIC VIEW

When padmas lose touch with their inherent joy, they become desolate. This disappointment can be fearsome. Padma's fiery energy lures, but it can also kill, like the flame that incinerates the moth. Padma people want their world hot, spicy, and emotional. Their passionate, intense desires can turn into obsessive clinging, like a love affair that consumes the lovers so they can't think of anything else. Padma performers reach such peaks when they are "on" that life feels flat and meaningless between performances. Being preoccupied by desire produces a kind of stupidity that fails to distinguish between grasping and destroying.

Padma people are extremely sensitive to the presence or absence of vitality. They long for intimacy if there is not enough, yet feel threatened if there is too much. Neurotic padmas continually question how close is comfortable. They embrace until they feel claustrophobic; then they reject. Another neurotic padma pattern is to grasp the moment and hold on to it, freezing it solid. Ironically the grasping kills the object of their desire. Paradoxically it dulls the intensity they seek. After a short lull, however, their energy erupts, and the cycle of grasping starts again. These patterns of push and pull, passion and aggression, love and hate, are the neurotic padmas' effort to manipulate their world to avoid pain and seek pleasure.

Fickle and easily distracted, padmas develop a relationship and then move on if it becomes too uncomfortable. They don't want to get stuck, because then the "magic" will disappear. Like ratnas, they never seem to get enough, but whereas ratnas milk the situation, padmas move on. They are gullible and easily seduced. Padmas are ambivalent about the world. It's hard to predict what they'll do next, because they're fluid, too slippery to pin down. They stick with something only if it is inherently exciting and involves people—like being a tour guide of exotic places.

Neurotic padmas are overly concerned with relationships, because fundamentally they feel incomplete, eternally separated from their lover and the world. They are always falling madly in love, only to end up heartbroken. They see someone else as wonderful and, feeling insignificant themselves, try to merge with that person. Because their sense of insufficiency creates the desire to possess, they are tremendously competitive. Like fire, they want to consume everything. They love the agony and the ecstasy of conquest and rejection, excitement and loss. They are the hot lovers of our world: sensual, coquettish, and seductive. They enjoy the touchy-feely and sometimes even the kinky. They can be erotomaniacs, seeking more and more erotic sensation. For extreme padmas the element of danger heightens the intensity. This energy can become manipulative and heartless.

Neurotic padmas constantly seek entertainment and excitement; boredom and mediocrity are threatening. When nothing is happening in their lives, padmas panic. They have very active minds, often wild and discursive. They can easily become overwhelmed by fantasies about new situations. They search for perfection and become irritable when they don't find it. "Is this all there is?" they ask. They are picky and fussy about whom and what they relate to, always making petty comparisons and being critical. Padmas have difficulty making decisions, because there are so many interesting yet potentially painful alternatives. Choosing one means forgoing all the others. Although they hate to miss out on any source of pleasure and excitement, they are also afraid of getting hurt.

The confusion created by this dilemma and the desolation of being alone make padmas prone to depression. They might also become manic in extreme cases. They take the edge off loneliness and depression by dwelling on the past and fantasizing about the future. Pain and pleasure become interchangeable; the pain is pleasurable because it is so intense. They use overindulgences of all kinds—drugs, drinking, and even being brokenhearted—as ways of forgetting or soothing the pain as well as heightening it.

The alternation between excitement and depression creates a general tone of moodiness in padmas. They wear their emotions on their sleeve. They take everything personally, so they are touchy and easily triggered. When a situation they have invited turns unpleasant, they close off with anger. When their natural excitability is repressed or overwhelmed, their energy becomes violent and fiery, as in a lovers' quarrel. They can become hysterical.

Neurotic padmas tend to be superficial and easily distracted. They think with a fluidity that can get them lost. They can become caught up in a succession of unrelated details that lack coherence. Then they seem scatterbrained, rambling, and meandering, like bubbly young girls who don't finish their sentences. Their fuzzy thinking can lead them into a traffic jam of discursive thought and baffle those around them.

Possible health problems for padmas include high blood pressure, caused by too much mental activity and overly intense emotions. Because they accumulate energy, they can't settle, which often leads to insomnia and obsessive sexual fantasies. Their tendency toward too rich a diet can be remedied by physical activity, which also provides calmer ground and more space.

Padma people take pleasure in the intensity of the hidden, reveling in the excitement of an illicit affair, the secret rendezvous, the intimate conversation. They like to hide mementos in secret places, keep a journal tucked under the mattress. In some cultures hidden things are part of the social order. The geisha women of Japan, for instance, live in their own enclaves. Men visit these houses as a matter of course but never speak of it to their wives. In the Ottoman Empire harem women were locked away from the rest of society and guarded by eunuchs. The harems constituted the sultans' private treasury of padma energy. Though these traditions are dying out, similar elements exist in many cultures.

Padmas have the ability to live outside societal norms because of their naturally eccentric behavior. They are perpetually indecisive and consult therapists, astrologers, gurus, or tarot cards to tell them what to do. They tend not to take the advice, however, because it feels too solid. They live in a world of adolescence—rebelling against authorities and following their peers.

The desire to please is so insidious that padma people often appear superficial and frivolous. But padmas have a natural ability to seduce and manipulate to get what they want; they know how to hook people. They want to con the world. They're perpetually friendly, sugary sweet, ingratiating. Appearance, glamour, and style rule over substance. As Professor Higgins says of women in *My Fair Lady*, padmas would rather fix their hair than fix up the mess inside their heads.

TRANSFORMING NEUROSIS INTO SANITY

The basic nature of padmas is to feel the intensity and preciousness of each moment. They oscillate between neurotic, clinging passion and an ability to communicate very accurately with the world because it is so immediate to them. So to transmute neurosis into sanity, padmas need to work with the energy of passion, a hunger to be close to the objects of their desire.

Amber is very much in love with Charles, but to her it seldom feels reciprocated. Her desire to be with him is continually frustrated. Every time it seems that they are not going to spend time together, she gets panicky. Her whole world begins to crumble; she feels she will never have what she wants with him. On the one hand, she gets angry; on the other hand, she grasps for any sense of connection with him. Hers is very much the padma pattern of push and pull.

To Amber her expectations seem appropriate. To Charles it always feels as if she wants too much togetherness. It takes many years in this relationship for them to see their patterns and each other. At some point Amber realizes that when all she feels is her need for him, she is actually blind to Charles himself. But when she stops grasping, she is intuitively perceptive about their relationship; she has a keen sense of the play of energies between them. She can be sensitive to him, feel compassionate toward him, and have her own feelings, too. When she stops clinging, she can discriminate between what is hers and what is his and feel each perspective genuinely.

Padma energy is associated with the human realm. Because padmas thrive on communicating and possess a discriminating intelligence, they are more able than other families to see and transcend their neurotic behavior. They finally realize that they have been playing the same role too long and begin to lose faith in it. When the "movie" becomes repetitive and familiar, padmas can open to new possibilities.

PADMA ACTIVITIES

To have an experiential sense of the quality of the padma family, choose from the following suggested activities. Appendix A, "The Five Wisdom Energies at a Glance," presents additional aspects of the family, which you could use to devise your own activities. Be creative.

- Dress in clothes with warm colors and soft textures that make you feel attractive. Wear clothes that reveal the lines of your body or flow as you move. Wear ornamentation—a tie or jewelry—that has special significance for you or might be a conversation starter.
- Decorate your living space or an area in your workplace by adding a flower arrangement, candles, or a particularly beautiful object and placing it in an appropriate spot.
- Pay attention to your emotional tone. Note when you feel gloomy, nostalgic, or lonely. Note how you react to others.

- Listen to music that is warm, sad, playful, or romantic. Play your favorites over and over again. Hum the tunes.
- Listen to someone speaking and see whether the words used correspond to his or her emotional tone. Note the person's style, rhythm, gestures, looks. Notice how you talk to different people.
- Purposefully use words and phrases like "me," "I like," "I can't stand," " I feel," "I want." See how they affect your experience of yourself.
- Read a short story, a novel, a magazine, or a book of poems. Notice what moves you.
- Give yourself plenty of time to fantasize about people you know or imagine and the circumstances of being with them.
- Enjoy communicating with people and engaging intimately with the world.

7

Karma: Activity

WISDOM ASPECT, SANE POSSIBILITIES

The wisdom of karma energy is all-accomplishing action, the completion of whatever needs to be done. At their best karma people do things effortlessly and appropriately. They are synchronized with the world, in harmony with all activity. Karma is associated with the color green and the element wind.

Karmas delight in movement and industry. Their genius lies in coordinating and juggling many projects at once. With their clear sense of direction, their action has coherence. They sense the movement in a situation and go with the flow. They know what to do, how to do it, when to act, and when to refrain from acting. They know what works. Their actions arise naturally and spontaneously. They involve themselves directly with whatever they do, putting thought into action without hesitation. Karma epitomizes a masculine approach to life—straightforward and practical, pragmatic and utilitarian.

Karmas are stable and happy, vivacious and full of positive energy. They exude confidence and are at ease with their own abilities. Karmas exhibit tremendous enthusiasm and exertion. They get exhilarated and inspired by what they do. Rather than barging through with a steamroller, they lubricate situations to bring about desired results. Karma people may not have many ideas or a sophisticated philosophy, but they can move the world forward.

Karmas' passion is power. They seek to control by direct action, but their intentions are benevolent. They work unselfishly for the good of all. Their drive to achieve is not based on desire for territory but on positioning themselves so they can strategically be more effective. They are aware that the more light-handed their power, the more effective it is.

The karma environment is characterized by dynamic activity that touches everything around it. Plans are made, schedules created, and goals accomplished, without obstruction. Karmas remain in constant motion, emitting a kinetic energy that seems almost still, it is going so fast. Their speed is not speedy but has a steady quality, like white noise. Although their action is persevering and direct, it can be light, even playful, or—depending on the need—as forceful as a hammer. Picture the offices of a large daily newspaper, where enormous amounts of information are collected and ordered into the day's news with the ever-present driving force of the deadline. Picture a movie set with hundreds of people, each in a role, creating and then dissolving scene after scene. The director sits in the middle of it, master of all. An army sergeant, a construction foreman, an athlete, and a social activist all exhibit karma energy. So does a summer morning in a garden full of flowers, bees, and butterflies.

Since karma people don't use a lot of forethought, their actions are based on trial and error. Their thinking is utilitarian rather than visionary. They always use the most up-to-date technique. They determinedly work through obstacles and resistance. Karma people exude a sense of possibility. They know how to counteract and work with the force, cunning, and power of others by going around them, outmaneuvering them, destroying them, or simply letting them be. No one cons karmas; they have an intelligent paranoia.

Karma people do not fear failure and so are able to wait with composure for just the right moment to take action. Then they need little force; one stroke might be enough. Their action is stillness in motion, not stillness as opposed to motion. They are receptive to movement, as in martial arts. Their efficiency results from being synchronized with the world, so their actions can be calm and flexible, always in balance.

In relationship karmas make contact in a direct, even intimate way. They are straightforward and direct in communication. They have a tendency to push people to act but do it skillfully enough not to offend.

Karma people maintain a constant relationship with their environment, always interacting with it. They like the world to be firm so they can push up against it. They relate to space with forceful, forward movement. They build momentum in a certain direction, but they can also change direction quickly if that is needed.

Karmas accept the inevitability of death as necessary for new birth. They accept beginnings and endings, building and tearing down, creating and destroying. Destroying for them implies liberation, freedom. Karmas are quick to cut through what is superfluous, such as neurotic behavior.

The United States, Japan, China, the dictatorships of Hitler and Stalin, and all dominant countries display karma energy. Action art, political art, Mexican murals, and the expressionists reflect karma energy, as well as artists such as de Kooning, Pollock, and Escher. Pop art, op art, graffiti, filmmaking, and found-object art embody the karma fondness for the pragmatic and utilitarian. Karma-type architecture is found in sports centers, airports, and train and bus stations. Typical karma dance forms are jazz, aerobics, Jazzercise, rock video dance, tap dance, break dancing, and some African dance. Most sports and some party games display karma energy, particularly if they are competitive. Martial arts reflect karma energy at its best.

Karma-type literature is either functional or full of activity—adventure stories, political treatises, how-to manuals, and cartoons. Karma music is fast and well articulated, displaying a sense of fearlessness and brilliance. It could be speedy, jumpy, harsh, and even militant. The Talking Heads and contemporary rap are good examples of karma energy. Classical composers such as Penderecki, Stravinsky, Elliot Carter, Bartók, and the Ketjak monkey chant from Bali display this energy. The elemental karma sound is the forward-thrusting sound of *o* (o).

Karmas tend to forage for food: they raid the refrigerator or grab fast food instead of cooking a meal. Karma people can be addicted to the highs of caffeine and sugar. Animals that display karma energy are the beaver, ants, bees, roadrunners, woodpeckers, and humming-birds.

Spiritually karma people possess the most interest in doing good for others. Their zeal can lead them to be evangelical. They can get caught up in techniques for achieving higher realization and become goal-oriented, thus missing the point. They want a therapy that works quickly and efficiently, like transactional analysis, or that has action as its main modality, like behavioral or dance therapy. The focus on changing habits needs to be environmentally or physically supported for a karma type. A body therapy like Rolfing, which is penetrating and forceful, has this energy.

INTENSIFIED PATTERNS, NEUROTIC VIEW

In neurotic mode karmas are driven by a need for action. They are overly energetic, restless, and speedy. Like gusting wind, they move haphazardly and indiscriminately and are impatient if they are inter-rupted or blocked. They panic, as if to say "Do something, do some-thing." They frantically create tasks. They live with perpetual nervous tension from constantly moving. They fear stillness; it's move or die. They rely on busyness to relieve their anxiety; activity acts as a pacifier. If they don't move, their minds just spin faster and faster with overlapping mental chatter. Eventually they lurch out of control—like a production line gone haywire or a windup toy that never stops. Since their discursiveness has little to do with the situa-tion at hand, in extreme cases they become psychotic.

Karma people have a preoccupation with power and control; they want to dominate others. They manipulate the world toward those ends. They seek power through deals, alliances, and compromises. They feel a need to get the world before it gets them. Since they must appear competent, they are never unprepared; they always know what to do. They both envy and resent those above them. They seek to establish checks and balances to make sure no one gets too much power.

Karmas are tremendously ambitious, which intensifies their need for control and concentration. They are always involved in many projects at once, so they develop strategies to cover all the bases. They don't want to miss out on anything, because it might threaten their position.

Because of their speed, neurotic karmas lack a synchronization of intention and action. They don't take time for reflection, so they lose sight of both the context of their actions and the end result. They impulsively push ahead for fear of falling behind. In trying too hard, they become inefficient. Their life is full of chaos.

Neurotic karmas exist in a milieu of insecurity and paranoia, seeing the world "out there" as trying to undermine and destroy them. Jealousy and envy come to the fore. Karma energy flourishes in the jealous god realm, which is full of rivalry and competition. Jealous gods are devious, deceptive, and calculating. Their ultimate fear is being incompetent or inadequate, being left out or losing track.

Neurotic karmas lack an expansive perspective. They do just what is in front of them, relying on tunnel vision. They become withdrawn, laboring with their nose to the grindstone, overly concerned about missing a detail. They mistakenly attempt to apply details or techniques universally. They are constantly trying to organize, reorder, tie up loose ends. Karma energy is goal-oriented, so it can be excessively pragmatic. Karmas lack spontaneity and so create a tedious, uniform world.

When karmas feel incompetent, they procrastinate. Their fear of failure is acute, so it blocks and saps their energy. They avoid challenges and become lazy or spaced out. Their resistance to activity generates exhaustion. In extreme cases their fear of failure could be so strong that they sacrifice their lives to keep their sense of honor— like the martial code of honor of the samurai. Here vajra's strong sense of principle combines with karma's need to do something. There are standards by which to live; if you can't uphold them, you die for them.

Their need to control can make karmas insensitive to the welfare of others, who become mere objects to be manipulated, tools to get the job done. They are impatient and disdainful of weakness or lack of ambition in others. They like to associate with people who are as responsible, dependable, and competent as they are.

Because neurotic karma people are paranoid and high-strung, relationships with them tend to get polarized into dramatic confrontations. The possibility of real communication is limited, because they don't trust anyone. Karmas interpret communication as an attack. They are heavy-handed and demanding. They flame up in anger when things are not going their way. They are harsh and curt; they divide the world into allies and enemies. They take pride in relying on their street smarts, on not getting caught. The police and the CIA exhibit karma energy.

Aggressive, speedy, and powerful, karmas take on strenuous tasks that require tremendous stamina. Then they burn out. They proceed full speed ahead and then drop dead—most likely from a heart attack. They are type A, stress-prone people.

As lovers, karma people are direct, forceful, and potent. They can be insensitive, brutish, manipulative—and potentially violent. Rape is an expression of this energy.

TRANSFORMING NEUROSIS INTO SANITY

The basic nature of karmas is activity. Sometimes they speedily accomplish one thing after another, driven by the paranoid sense that others might get ahead of them; other times their actions are spontaneous and meet the needs of the moment. By relaxing their drive and ambition and learning to trust their own abilities, they can transmute their energy into wisdom.

Ralph and Lisa—two visionary, hardworking, and powerful people—had helped to establish a small organization. However, the relationship between Ralph as manager and Lisa as an employee with investments in the company was soon fraught with tension. Ralph felt driven to accomplish and charged ahead without consulting others. Lisa was often outspoken about how matters should be handled, which felt threatening to Ralph. Though originally they were supportive of each other, what developed was an underlying current of distrust and paranoia. Whereas Ralph was oblivious to it, Lisa was often anguished that their relationship lacked a sense of ease. At the same time she was amazed at Ralph's brilliance and respected him for the way he took command in all aspects of their organization.

Things didn't shift until Lisa realized the extent to which her lack of trust was creating the tension. Painful as it was to acknowledge, she saw how solidified her view had become. She relaxed her paranoia and began to trust the situation. She stopped competing for control and attempting to impose her view of "the right way to do things," and instead confined herself to her areas of expertise. She worked on having a friendly, no-agenda relationship with Ralph. Every time he exhibited paranoia by words or deeds, she let his behavior slide without buying into it. She transmuted her own competitiveness and began to appreciate his style. That allowed Ralph to relax, feel confident, and accomplish in a more effortless way.

KARMA ACTIVITIES

To experience the quality of the karma family, choose from the following suggested activities. You might find more ideas for activities by looking at appendix A, "The Five Wisdom Energies at a Glance."

- Wear practical clothes that allow you to move freely. Stick to muted colors. No need for ornamentation. Make sure you wear a watch.
- Organize yourself: make appointments and schedule activities for the day and week. Make lists of things to do. Budget your time and money.
- Decide on a sport or physical activity that interests you and start doing it.
- Have a quick meal while trying to do something else at the same time, like talking on the phone or working at your computer.
- Clean and organize your house or workplace. Wash the windows; clean out the basement. Organize closets or file drawers. Rearrange the furniture.
- Fix things in your house that need repair.
- Read the manuals for all your appliances to see how they work.
- Watch people in a busy train station, an airport, a factory loading dock, or a warehouse.
- Enjoy accomplishing things.

8

Buddha: Spaciousness

WISDOM ASPECT, SANE POSSIBILITIES

The wisdom of buddha energy is a sense of all-pervasive space—vast, boundless, and wakeful. As the most fundamental energy, buddha provides the space for all the other energies to manifest. It is completely alive and awake without purpose or direction—an awareness that has no bias. It has a sense of just being in fundamental peace. It is existence itself. It accommodates nothing and everything, emptiness and fullness.

The symbol of buddha energy is a wheel or circle, encompassing all. It is associated with the element of space and the color white, luminous and pure. Like a prism or a rainbow, it includes all the colors rather than identifying with just one. This energy has a sense of timelessness: as all things arise, so all things pass.

The environment of the buddha family is like a great plain, a desert, or a snow field, where land and sky merge with each other in the vastness of open space. It is silent and still. Nothing is happening. A primordial peace pervades the space. The barren landscape has no obvious features; it is simply vast, empty, undefined. Like the ancient ruins of a temple, a ghost town, or a recently vacated campground, it is pervaded by a sense of absence. In this primordial space—

without a when or a where—our consciousness can expand all the way to infinity.

For people with a pronounced buddha quality, life can be blissful and satisfyingly simple. These people seem to be imbued with a contemplative or meditative presence. They possess a rounded wholesomeness without sharp boundaries. Not much happens in their world. On the one hand, they can seem plain and ordinary. On the other hand, they have a genius for living profoundly straightforward lives. With no place to "go" and nothing to "do," they can just "be." They don't get caught up in speed and ambition or become preoccupied with petty concerns.

Buddha people are not very expressive, nor do they have much desire to communicate. They are passive and receptive. Their quality of spaciousness is completely accommodating. Because they are willing to include everything, they see the whole picture without taking sides. They exhibit a sense of inclusiveness and appreciation. Surprises don't ruffle them, because they have seen it all. They are grounded and easygoing. Everything is OK. Since they have no agenda and do not try to manipulate situations, they have an anchoring quality. Sometimes they seem to be the only people who manage to stay calm in a tumultuous situation. Their power lies in being rooted and resting in the essence. They can align with the world and be in harmony with it, in touch with the basic forces of nature in an elemental way.

Buddha people are inquisitive, possessing a sense of awe and wonder. They exist in a moment-to-moment nowness. They tend to lose track of details, because things don't weigh heavily on them. They sense that, ultimately, no issue is really that serious, nothing really matters. Since they take the path of least resistance, they are comfortable doing repetitive work that might seem tedious to others. They are persevering, so they provide a sense of continuity.

When buddha people become active, they take on the quality of one of the other types. Buddhas with vajra energy have a spacious clarity, which is not as sharp as vajra alone. They are stable and have a broad view. Ratna can add an earthy richness and enjoyment to the basic energy of buddha. Padma adds immediacy, intimacy, and friendliness. Buddha mixed with karma is powerful and direct.

Buddha people exude a sense of humility. They lack self-consciousness and do not idealize: they are who they are. Passion and aggression are not evident in this type. Because they see the big picture, they tend not to struggle with their lives. They are often cheerful, believing that the world is good. They radiate a childlike naïveté and a playful innocence.

Buddha is often the dominant energy in spiritual teachers and peasants. They dress in simple, muted colors and speak slowly and directly. Buddha energy shows up in tribal cultures and those based on philosophies of simplicity, like the Amish.

Because buddha types are not driven to express themselves, buddha-family art, when created, is minimalist. Eastern art forms contain a strong contemplative component, both in the process of creation and in the spaciousness of the result. Japanese art forms like the tea ceremony, *bugaku* (court dance), brush painting, and haiku poetry are examples. Dance forms can be fast and active and still evoke spaciousness, like the whirling dervishes of the Sufi tradition and the American Indian dances. Repetitious chanting and some modern music, like that of composers Philip Glass or Steve Reich, express buddha energy by creating a sense of vastness lacking much definition. Brian Eno is a contemporary composer who does this masterfully. The elemental sound of buddha energy is a long, drawn-out *ah* that resonates through the head.

Buddha types learn by repetition and by reducing the subject to its basic concepts. They learn by osmosis rather than in a linear way. Buddhas move slowly in making decisions: a response might take days, weeks, or months. They like the idea of sleeping on a question.

In terms of sports or physical activities, buddha people might take to fishing. They could get immense satisfaction just sitting there waiting for something to happen. A macrobiotic diet, eating relatively bland foods like tofu and rice, is typical of a buddha approach to food. Buddhas might even forget to eat.

Psychotherapy with a buddha-family orientation would be client-centered, like Rogerian work, with its focus on establishing a genuine relationship, conveying empathy and an unconditionally positive regard for the client. Contemplative psychotherapy, in which the therapist could make minimal interventions allowing a lot of compassionate space, also exemplifies buddha energy. Buddha types gravitate toward basic, slow forms of self-cultivation, like breath therapy. They might even prefer something less interactive, like sitting meditation. As people grow old, they naturally tend to have more buddha energy, becoming slower and more enamored of routine.

INTENSIFIED PATTERNS, NEUROTIC VIEW

Though buddha energy has the potential to be open and accommodating, it also can become solidified and closed down. Of all the energy families, it manifests the most sane and the most neurotic tendencies. In its neurotic manifestation, ignoring, avoiding, and denying become the way to keep from experiencing uncertainty and change, the way to create a safe, familiar world.

Buddha people fear the unknown and want their world to be simple and predictable. Their lives can become very repetitive, sticking to the same routines every day. They reduce the parameters of their world so it becomes small and safe. They get mired in inertia. They play deaf, dumb, and blind.

They don't want to relate directly to the details of life. They take jobs that require little effort. They exclude what gets in their way, internally or externally, dulling themselves so they don't notice other possibilities. They say, "I'm tired," or "I don't know." Their slogan is, "It will take care of itself."

All this ignoring takes great effort. First you have to notice everything, and then you have to deliberately choose to turn away from it. Buddha people have lots of thoughts that are undirected and fleeting. They tend to be forgetful, absorbed in their own world, closed into themselves. They dull their sense perceptions to minimize contact with their environment. In extreme cases a buddha person can be catatonic, living in a frozen world.

Even when life feels OK, buddha types experience a pervasive anxiety about losing ground or falling apart. They know that ultimately there is nothing to hold on to, so they worry about survival and continually attempt to secure themselves. They try to make everything peaceful, but this invites the anxiety of emptiness. Paradoxically impermanence can become a refuge for buddha types, who reason that, "However bad it is, it won't last forever."

To other people buddha types often seem invisible, as if they were wearing camouflage. They are rarely noticed in a group. They like uneventful relationships. They display dull, neutral emotions. As lovers, they like repetition. They can't be bothered with trying to talk anyone into anything. Even if they're lonely, they usually wait for other people to seek them out. People are attracted to them because they provide plenty of space onto which to project!

The characteristic neurosis of each of the other energy types gets heightened by mixing with the denseness of neurotic buddha energy. Buddha neurosis manifests in either the animal realm or the god realm—like a rat in a maze or a god on a cloud. In the animal realm people who are extremely buddha are stony and stubborn. They refuse to see alternatives and relate only to what is in front of them. They are lazy and slothful and lack a sense of humor. They are preoccupied, dull, and rigid. They repeat the same thoughts, the same activities, with the same people. Neurotic buddha tinged with neurotic vajra clarity has a more impenetrable quality than vajra alone. These people are exceptionally rigid and narrow-minded; they stick to tradition. They are self-righteous and want to be acknowledged as being right. They condemn anyone with a different view. Buddha mixed with ratna enrichment becomes heavy and oppressive, overly territorial, wallowing in self-indulgence. Mixed with padma passion, buddha is too "familiar," exuding a pseudointimacy. Such people can lose track of themselves, not remembering where they are or what they are doing. Buddha with karma activity is more stubborn and insensitive than pure karma, which is more manipulative. It can be aggressive and tough like a bulldozer, pushing obstacles out of the way without regard for the effect on others.

In the god realm—the other place neurotic buddha energy manifests—the buddha family is spacious to a fault. Absorbed in self-satisfied bliss, gods don't want to get involved, so they just watch what's going on. Buddha/vajra people in the god realm are fascinated by, and arrogant about, their own brilliance. They like to outsmart others. The ratna element brings a self-satisfied complacency to buddha. Surrounded by ever-increasing material comforts, buddha/ratnas command the royal seat. Buddha/padmas are intoxicated with pleasure and perpetually seek more. They like to get high, blissed-out, and are constantly exclaiming how wonderful things are. They are narcissistic as well as charming. Buddha/karma people have more perspective and intelligence in the god realm than in the animal realm, so they wield more power and control. They can see where people's weaknesses lie and how to undermine, intimidate, and impress them.

Because buddha neurosis exists in a self-contained system, resisting change or any input from the outside, it is the hardest of all the five energies to penetrate. It refuses to acknowledge that there is a problem. Buddha people tend to either muddle through or become proud and complacent. Because they are numb both to their own pain and to the pain of the world, they feel little motivation for change.

TRANSFORMING NEUROSIS INTO SANITY

Buddha's basic nature is a sense of being still and pacifying. A buddha teeters between seeing the world as solid and seeing it as spacious. When the world is felt to be solid, it is threatening. The tendency is to withdraw, avoid, deny. When it is experienced as spacious, all is accommodated: there is no problem.

When Chris is overwhelmed by the demands of the world, he stubbornly refuses to relate to the world outside himself. He experiences other people, the demands of his job, and the activity around him as pressure, a solid world closing in on him. He can even experience intimacy—as with his wife and children—as a threat. It is all too much. He wants life simple. He creates an inner world, a cocoon, that is sufficient unto itself.

With prodding from his wife, Chris begins to recognize his patterns. He reminds himself—or his wife reminds him—to open at just the point when he wants to close. With this awareness he finds that it is not so very difficult to accommodate what is going on around him. The space is full, but it is also empty. When Chris relaxes, although he still ignores the various possibilities life presents, he experiences a sense of spaciousness. It is not that he relates more to his world; it's that he accommodates it. He no longer sees it as threatening.

BUDDHA ACTIVITIES

To have an experiential sense of the quality of the buddha family, choose from the following suggested activities.

- Wear simple clothes in muted colors and no ornamentation. Wear the same clothes every day.
- In general do as little as possible: sit and do nothing for as long as you can, take a slow walk, spend a day in your pajamas, have the TV on without particularly paying attention to it.
- Eat simple food and stick to the same menu every day.
- Don't bother to tidy up your house.
- Have a conversation and leave pauses between the words, the sentences.
- Enjoy the spaciousness that this energy provides.

PART TWO

MANDALA: THE ENERGETIC MATRIX

9

Our Mix of Colors

As in a rainbow, prism, or kaleidoscope, mandala is the constant play of the five energies. In this chapter we will explore the idea of mandala principle as a way of working with ourselves. Seeing our inner world as a mandala deepens our understanding of who we are and helps us transcend the illusions that (1) we are only one color and (2) we are separate from others. In chapter 11 we will see how, with the perspective of mandala, we can open to the reality of a vast world of interconnected energies.

OUR UNIQUE COLOR MIX

We are born with certain energies. Others we learn. Still others arise as we adapt to life. When we become aware of the mix of colors in ourselves, we can no longer identify exclusively with one energy. Defining ourselves as a padma or a ratna solidifies and centralizes our sense of who we are. By narrowing our range, we box ourselves in and miss the play of totality.

The rich fabric of our being contains threads of many colors. Some are bold highlights; others are more subtle. In the best of situations, these colors complement one another. At other times they are discordant and chaotic, out of balance: the blue is too bright, the green too dark, the red too intense. The five energies are constantly shifting. When we see our mix of colors, we realize that our energies are difficult to pin down. We see how interconnected and layered they are. Recognizing how changeable our experience is takes the "I" out of it. Aware of all the colors, open to all the aspects of our own being, we can move freely from one energy to another. We can function impartially and relate to the total situation rather than latching onto one narrow perspective.

Curious about the five wisdom families, Claudine chose to practice for a week with each energy. She describes her experience:

> I became truly aware, for the first time, of what it means to lean into the "energy of the moment." Because each family evoked such definite and distinct responses in terms of mind content, feelings, and physical reactions, I realized more clearly where I was stuck and which energies I wanted and needed to cultivate. Two insights were particularly precious: the realizations that (a) buddha accommodates all experiences and that in that sense everything is workable, and (b) the purposeful ability to act (karma) is possible in my situation (that is, unemployment). . . . The week I worked with vajra, I had a job interview and did manifest a greater clarity and logical thinking in preparing for it and carrying it out. The week I did padma, I started as a volunteer on the sexual-assault crisis line. I felt a very direct and heart-piercing compassion during some of my calls—as opposed to sympathy or empathy. Throughout my practice of karma, I experienced a sense of simply "feeling good" and "safe" such as I had not experienced in a very long while. As well as experiencing some of the sane energy, I also experienced some neurosis in each, as follows: unfulfilled sexual arousal with buddha; fear of coldness, distance, and anger with vajra; financial anxieties with ratna; sadness and depression with padma; and restlessness with karma.

Once when I was doing the self-visualization exercise at the end of chapter 1, I saw myself as a landscape: a meadow with spring blossoms everywhere. What I chose as my "partner" was a vast snowy mountainscape. What do these qualities mean to me? What is my meadow, and why would I gaze longingly at mountain peaks? My spontaneous insight was that this picture was a metaphor for the energies that often exist in the relationship with my husband. I often feel like inviting a sense of padma pleasure and enjoyment that one could experience in nature on a spring day. However, I find that I am equally attracted to the towering peaks of vajra intellect and high ideals that I experience in his energy.

RECOGNIZING OUR STYLE

The buddha families are neutral. It is our relationship to them that determines whether we manifest as confused or awake. Recognizing our style has to do with paying close attention to our habitual patterns from day to day, moment to moment, in different situations. The confusion is where we get stuck. It's the wall we keep running into. The sanity is our skill, our brilliance. In the beginning we tend to have a dualistic view: we want to avoid our confusion and cling to what feels more genuine or authentic.

However, it is only when we appreciate both the sane and neurotic qualities of our experience that we can fully understand how we embody the energies. Full awareness of the spectrum of the energies gives us the power to view our experience in an unbiased, nonjudgmental way. We are not trying to change or fix ourselves but to relate wholeheartedly to our mix of colors, however intense or subdued.

To begin working with the energies on an inner level, it is helpful to contemplate the descriptions of the families in chapters 4–8, which encompass the full spectrum of experience from darkness to brilliance. As you practice working with the energies by exploring the awareness exercises at the end of each chapter, you may find that insights arise. In practicing these exercises, you are experiencing the energies in the moment. You are seeing or feeling the world directly. When insight arises, just let it be. Remember to notice your breathing. Don't jump to conclusions. Don't elaborate or analyze. Remain open. This is how to work with your innate intelligence rather than just trying to fit yourself into a system. As you work with the energies, it is also good to take note of feedback from others. We are often the last to know who we are.

As you become aware of your own play of energies, you'll see that one of the energies is basic to your being. This is the dominant energy of your unique mandala. For some people there can be two dominant energies. You'll also notice that other energies—called enhancement energies, mask energies, and complementary energies— arise under particular circumstances. Enhancement energy and mask energy are ways in which you "exit" from your dominant energy. The enhancement energy is one you use to embellish or adorn your basic way of being; the mask energy is one you use to hide it. Complementary energy is what you seek in others to balance out your own energy.

DOMINANT ENERGIES

Most of us have one or two energy families that are fundamental to us. They are intrinsic to our basic nature—the style that characterizes our perspective, physical being, speech patterns, and thoughts. These are the dominant energies. They can manifest alone or in combination with another energy. For example, our dominant energy might be vajra in combination with either buddha, ratna, padma, or karma. To illustrate: Rob, a history professor who is writing a book, is predominately vajra/ratna. He has the brilliant clarity of the overview and the rich resources to include much fascinating detail.

For some people the dominant energy is obvious; for others the dominant energy is more hidden. For example, my own dominant energy feels to me like a primal stream, as if I have been this way for a long time. The dominant family is where we feel familiar, at home. It might not be the most pleasant or the most interesting place, but it's what we know best. In our dominant energy we manifest both our sanity and our confusion.

One way to cultivate awareness of our dominant energy is to look at deeply ingrained habitual patterns. The dominant energy will show up in how we want the world to be—hot or cool, many-colored or black-and-white, rich or sparse, exciting or calm. It will also show up in thoughts of "I want this" or "I feel this." Our dominant emotional tone is another strong indication of our basic energy. (We will take a more detailed look at emotions and their corresponding families in chapter 13.)

For some people the dominant energy is a safe place to be, but in a situation that demands another energy, they become confused. For example, a vajra person might be perfectly sane in a vajra situation, but given a padma situation to deal with, the vajra displays a lot of neurosis.

I find that I can tune in to someone's dominant quality quickly in a brief telephone conversation, even if I've never met the person before. For example, when I telephoned a busy professional to make a request, I got a sharp retort, "No." He then launched into a lengthy, detailed explanation of why what I had requested was impossible. I got a strong hit of vajra energy. Because my question was a threat to how he viewed his world, he erected a strong boundary: "No." In another instance, when an acquaintance told me more than I wanted to know about her personal life situation and her need for help, I felt myself entering the ratna family.

There are many aspects to each energy, so even when people have the same dominant energies, their individual display will be unique. Karl and Rachel are both career-oriented karma types who hold responsible jobs in the movie industry. Karl is a director; his karma energy tends to have a lot of force. As a costume designer, Rachel works quietly but diligently in the background. Since they both also have strong padma energy, they have lots of friends and are invited to many parties. However, whereas Karl's padma is extroverted and actively engaging, Rachel tends to favor quiet, intimate conversations. Though both have dominant karma/padma energy, their psychological orientations and way of being in the world are quite different.

EXIT ENERGY

Psychological shifts of energy from the dominant family to a subfamily are called "exits." Each of us has our favorite place to go, our favorite way to exit our basic energy pattern. We can exit by using another energy as an enhancement—a way of embellishing who we are. This could be seen as our "sane" way to exit. Or we can exit by using another energy as a mask—a way of concealing ourselves. This could be seen as our "confused" way to exit. Whereas our dominant energy family is consistent, the energies we use as exits are changeable, depending on the circumstances.

It is possible for someone to be stuck in his or her dominant energy, unable to exit. Being limited to just one energy, people like this are somewhat dysfunctional. This is often true of buddha people who are so self-absorbed that they see no way out. They don't bother to lift their gaze.

Enhancement

In our basic nature we are naked. With our enhancement energy, we put on clothes to fit the occasion. Sometimes the enhancement energy blends with our dominant family. For example, the enhancement energy might mix with the dominant energy to create our persona, the face we show to the world. If our basic energy is vajra and our enhancement energy is padma, our way of being in the world might be to magnetize with intellect. In contrast, if we are predominantly vajra with a buddha enhancement, we would stay in an ivory tower. This is how the exit as enhancement works. It's a way of embellishing who we are, adorning ourselves, in order to relate sanely to another energy. There can be much intelligence in our choice of enhancement energy. For example, if we grew up in a family in which a particular energy was dominant—or encountered a particular dominant energy at school—we learned to use that energy to enhance our dominant mode of being as a way to fit in.

June's dominant energy is a mix of vajra clarity and ratna wealth and creativity. In grade school she showed a high aptitude in all subjects—the highest test scores the principal had ever seen. However, in junior high her work did not reflect this aptitude. Since she didn't have to work hard to get good grades, she stopped applying herself. She became more interested in the social scene and embellished with padma, which is true of most teenagers in any case. June didn't begin to shine until she entered a private school where her intellect and creativity were supported and being smart was the norm. She also never stopped partying. It was easier to be herself in the new situation.

Vajra is an energy that I have cultivated as an enhancement. (In addition, some vajra has rubbed off on me through my relationship with my husband, in whom it is a dominant energy.) As a choreographer, I found I had a certain amount of vajra. However, what brought it out most strongly was my passion to study Buddhism. Later, vajra energy enabled me to be clear in teaching and to have an overview in big projects and leadership situations. Sometimes I use my vajra color as a way of getting people to take me seriously.

Some styles are more acceptable than others in a particular culture. Because our society appreciates karma, people often take this energy on as an enhancement in order to survive. They learn to hold a nine-to-five job, have kids, take care of the domestic situation, maintain numerous material possessions, and go on a vacation annually. This amount of activity is considered normal in Western society. We may feel the need to cultivate the "let's do it" quality of karma to live here. If the energy isn't basic to us, we might feel conflicted. However, we may be able to develop and refine it as enhancement energy in a sane way. If it allows us to go beyond our comfort zone, the effort may be worth it.

Padma energy creates an interesting twist on exits. People often cultivate padma energy as the way to be in a social situation. However, when padma energy leads to an illicit relationship, it is usually kept hidden. Then one's dominant energy actually masks padma energy. For example, a married vajra/ratna person becomes infatuated with a seductive padma person. In order to express his passion, he will have to be willing to lie in order to hide it from his wife. In this case the dominant (vajra/ratna) masks the exit (padma), and so becomes neurotic. In contrast, when passion is open and celebrated, as in a good partnership, it can enhance the dominant. Then padma is an enhancement.

Mask

If we have not made friends with our dominant energy, we will use other energies as a mask, a way of shielding ourselves or hiding from painful situations that our basic energy can't handle. We take on an exit as a mask because we are afraid to show our true self.

For instance, Joel is a karma person who is always concerned about appearing competent. Because he does not have what it takes in many situations, however, he uses padma energy to con people into thinking that he can do more than he can. He protects himself by being very padma, someone whom everyone enjoys. He never really acknowledges his basic karma energy because he is not comfortable with it. He has not made friends with himself. He prefers to be seen as padma, though an ambitious speed underlies it.

Since the mask is a pretense based on uncertainty or discomfort with ourselves, it is an expression of neurosis. We pretend to be something that we think will make us more acceptable to others. Operating from behind a mask can be exhausting. For example, Carolyn's basic energy is padma. But when her husband died, she become a busy karma to cover the intensity of her more emotional padma self. Only at the end of the day could she allow her feelings of loss and bereavement to emerge. Over the long months after his death, it became a relief to come "home" and be herself again.

Doris's family was into sports. They were all dominantly karma. Being dominantly ratna, Doris was more slow-moving and sedate, with a tendency to put on weight. In response to pressure from the family to be more active, she became anorexic. She exited to karma to fit in, but instead of becoming more active, she took on the energy by exerting extreme control in her eating habits. (Body issues are common with ratna people.)

Michele was padma as a child, a happy little girl whom everyone adored. During her school years she faced increasing demands to excel and accomplish more. She began to develop karma as a mask. As she grew into her teens, she was seen as a very functional karma person. She kept her padma, her basic energy, concealed. She had many boyfriends, whom she often kept secret. After she married, her husband also rejected her padma ways. Michele was never able to be herself, even in her closest relationships. Fortunately she found an outlet for her padma energy in becoming a successful artist.

Up to this point we have been talking about how exits can be a way of either propagating sanity (enhancement) or hiding it (mask). In fact, the same energy can be both an enhancement and a mask. A vajra person might take on a padma enhancement to go to his partner's parties, sometimes genuinely enhancing who he is. At other times he could use it as a cover, a mask—as in the false smile.

Here is an example of how I experience exiting as both enhancement and mask. When I was in the middle of a busy workday full of karma energy (which is basic to me), my daughter came home crying. Instantly I was the embracing, nurturing mother. I had switched to a padma/ratna mode as an enhancement. However, when she then continually interrupted me wanting to chat about this or that, I went to the boundary-setting energy of vajra: "I need to work now." When I am relaxed, it is easy to go to other energies as enhancement, embellishment. When my energy is constricted—I am on karma overdrive—I will more likely use a mask, a pretense, a cover. Then I might embrace my daughter but feel impatient and distracted while doing so. It feels as if I am faking it. Or I might snap at her with a series of justifications for why she can't interrupt me. At those times I am putting up a vajra mask.

Our way of exiting changes with the situation. For example, when I was a performer, an artist, and single, I had much more padma energy. When I married and had a family, my ratna came to the fore. When I moved into administrative work, I found vajra and karma more present in my life. Bringing sitting meditation into my life cultivated buddha energy. Whatever energy a particular situation demands will come out—unless, of course, we resist it.

COMPLEMENTARY ENERGY

Complementary energy is what we seek in others to balance our own energy. The styles of our partner and friends aerate our own. They act as a counterpoint to our energy and prevent us from sinking further into our neurosis, where we might get stuck. For example, I tend to get emotionally caught up and can't see things clearly (padma). My husband has the pacifying and clarifying qualities of vajra, which at times I find invaluable in navigating through my confusion.

Complementary energies ventilate or lubricate our whole situation. They are antidotes to our way of being. Seeking out complementary energy can be a way of taking a vacation from ourselves. As a hardworking businessman, for example, Neal likes nothing better than a night on the town with a fun-loving friend who puts him into a completely different world. Or sometimes he just wants to be with his partner, who meditates when the day is done.

Complementary energies can also provoke, threaten, irritate, and undermine. As much as we may appreciate someone else's energy when we are open to her, her entirely different perspective can be challenging. The complementary energy we see in another person might even be our own dominant energy that we lack the confidence to express. We might seek another's energy because it helps us experience ourselves more fully.

Whether they are healing or destructive, complementary energies have the power to puncture the solidity of our world. For example, Herald has a lot of "poor me" ratna. When he gets together with his close friend Bernard, he generally spends a lot of time whining. Bernard's buddha quality gives Herald the space to just play out his story line without feeding it. That way it loses its charge. This is healing, supportive. In contrast, Bernard's wife is very critical of Herald and can't stand his continually bemoaning his fate. This is a destructive relationship.

A classic example of a complementary relationship is the marriage between the intellectual vajra person and the sociable padma. Another is the ratna/karma alliance. Vajra and karma together don't work so well: the energy is too sharp and forceful. Padma and ratna together create energy that is overly emotional.

Throughout this chapter we have been looking at the facets of our inner mandala. Contemplate this information. Observe yourself. From time to time you might have insights about which quality or qualities seem basic to you and which might be your enhancement or mask. It doesn't really matter to which energy you relate at the beginning. When you become friends with any of your colors, the world opens. All routes lead into the totality. The basic instruction is, When insight arises, just let it be. Don't hang on to your insights as a way of solidifying yourself. Notice your breath. Remain open. This is how to work with your innate intelligence instead of just trying to fit yourself into a system.

EXERCISE: CREATING A PERSONAL MANDALA

Creating a personal mandala is a way of beginning to look at yourself and your life from the perspective of all five energies. Take some time to examine the different things you do in your daily life—in your home, your intimate relationships, your family, your job, school, recreation, and spiritual or self-awareness path. Feel the ambient tone, the energy, the quality or texture, the emotional space, the mind state that each of them brings up for you.

In Tibetan Buddhism a mandala is a circular graphic depiction of the five energies of a particular worldview. All five families are always represented. There is a center, and there are four directions. Buddha is generally in the center. If you are looking at the mandala in front of you, vajra is in front, ratna to the left side (going clockwise), padma at the back, and karma to the right. You can also imagine that you are in the center of this mandala, with vajra to your front, ratna to your right, padma in back, and karma to your left.

Whether you use this traditional visual format or play with others, begin to create a personal mandala. You can work with drawing, coloring, or making collages using pictures and personal objects that symbolize a particular quality for you. You could write poems for each family, and you could accompany the whole thing with song or music.

In the center put whatever in your life creates the most sense of space and accommodation for you. In the vajra direction put whatever helps you see clearly, whatever gives you a sense of vision or direction. In the ratna direction put whatever enriches your life, whatever gives it a sense of fullness. In the padma direction put whatever conveys a sense of communication or fluidity with your world and brings out your feelings. In the karma direction put whatever represents action and accomplishment.

The idea is to make your mandala a personal expression of who you are. It can be elaborate or simple, depending on your style. Revisit it from time to time. Watch it change and develop as you gain more intimacy with the colors of the families.

10

The Dynamics of Relationships

SEEING THE PATTERNS IN RELATIONSHIPS

I look across the breakfast table at my teenage daughter and think, How can she be of my blood and have come from my womb? I have lived with her for fifteen years, and yet she seems an enigma. I know what she likes for breakfast, when she goes to bed, and who her friends are. I have been through countless intimate situations from infancy to her first school days to dating, but there are times when I simply cannot believe what she says and does. Her world feels foreign to me. How can she remain such a mystery when I know her so well?

Mystery underlies all our relationships: with romantic partners, family members, coworkers, and the mailman. We can know someone on both superficial and deep levels, and yet we don't really understand him. Someone we've lived with, slept with, had children with can still have us wondering, Who are you?

In this chapter we will look at the dynamics of relationships, seeing how energetic patterns emerge and how we can work with them. We will also learn how to begin to recognize the dominant, enhancement, and mask energies that exist in our relationships, just as we saw how these energies exist within us. Cultivating awareness of the patterns of relationship in this way opens us to a larger mandala.

Opening to others' energies often feels confusing. Trying to find the place to connect with someone can feel very awkward. When we are aware of another person's colorings, we can begin to see that her energies have some predictability. This gives us a sense of what we can and cannot expect from her. It's how we learn to dance with each other. It doesn't mean that she will always act the same way. The same person will manifest differently in different situations. As humans, we are both predictable and surprising. However, by looking at the patterns in relationships, we can see how energies resist one another or merge. When they resist one another, we become closed and polarized. When they merge, we become open to each other's full palette of colors.

OPEN AND CLOSED

Any relationship contains both closed and open possibilities. Remember padma Jenny and buddha Steve, whom we met in the second chapter? They are a couple who complement each other nicely. Steve provides space for Jenny to bounce in; she needs space because she likes to bounce. She even gets Steve bouncing at times, which is just what he needs. So things work out fine—until Jenny gets bored with Steve's dullness, and Steve gets tired of Jenny's vivacious energy. Then Jenny bounces into bed—with another, more demonstrative man. Steve, meanwhile, has ignored Jenny's need for play and is oblivious to how sensual she has become lately. Jenny has tried to draw him out in her exuberant way, but the more she tries, the more sullen and withdrawn he becomes. They become polarized: Jenny's too clinging; Steve's too flat.

How can they work this out? Jenny might remember how much she likes Steve's accommodating style, which allows her so much room to be herself. She would probably burn out with a more exuberant man. Steve, on the other hand, might remember that he likes someone to perk him up at times; it's fun. They have to find where their styles complement each other.

At a more subtle level, something else is going on between Jenny and Steve. Steve has a vajra enhancement, and Jenny has a karma enhancement. When things get very difficult between them, Jenny makes sure they do something about it: she gets them talking. Jenny communicates about her emotions, which allows Steve to become more conversant with his own. Steve, on the other hand, provides some clarity about the patterns they create together. For instance, when Steve is too buddha, Jenny just wants to leave; when he engages her with his intellect, she is happy to be around. When Jenny is too busy, Steve withdraws more; when she wants to engage him in a playful way, he likes changing gears. So in this case their enhancements help to support the relationship, keeping it from getting too polarized.

Let's look at how a ratna type might be both open and closed. To most of his friends, George is a generous, warmhearted, intelligent, fun-loving guy who gives great parties. With his scholarly colleagues he is intellectually voracious, with his friends he always has new things to share, and with children he is full of entertaining stories. His house is constantly overflowing with people. From the outside this man might look like a good catch for any woman.

But George's life is so full that there is not much room in it for another person. Though George longs for an intimate relationship, he doesn't realize that he is not allowing space for one. Women come and go in his life. Although each relationship might be delightful while it lasts, the women eventually become claustrophobic. They suffocate either from an overabundance of affection or from George's rich diet of activity and people. It would take a spacious person indeed to be able to give George the amount of room he needs to be fully himself. It will be hard for George to find the intimacy he seeks because the solidity of his ratna does not allow padma.

Because George has a vajra enhancement, he takes great delight in pursuing intellectual projects. When he is wrapped up in his work, the more confusing aspect of his ratna self falls away. Then ratna joins with vajra to produce masses of papers, articles, and books. It is the intimacy he shares working on these projects with friends that he most enjoys.

THE PITFALL OF PROJECTING

We continually create our world through projections. This is especially easy to do in relationships. When we are working just with ourselves, we can sometimes find space to contemplate who we are. We can begin to see how we create our world by projecting our expectations and conditioning onto it. In relationship it is trickier, because we tend to react to other people. We project our expectations onto them and blame them for not living up to our projection. The trap of blame is like quicksand. Once we are in it, it is hard to get out; it keeps sucking us in. We start believing in our own story line. The trap of blame solidifies our negative energy. If we can see the energy dynamics in a situation—the inevitability that someone's tendencies will be heightened under certain circumstances—it is possible not to blame. What happens happens. Being aware of the five energies can help us practice looking at how we contribute to creating the mutual projection called a relationship. What is the energy that we bring to the situation?

When we try to "get what we want" from a relationship based on our desires and expectations, chances are we are projecting. We expect other people to be the way we think they are. Here is an example of a padma/karma mix that did not work. Allison and Alex struggled for years in their relationship. Alex wanted to merge; Allison did not. He wanted his version of her; she did not comply. He was continually astonished by her actions. He was always getting what he didn't want from her and not getting what he did want. His line always seemed to be, "Let's be intimate and affectionate," whereas hers was, "I've been working hard, and I'm tired." Wanting her to be sexy, he bought her alluring clothes that were merely an embarrassment to Allison, whose identity was wrapped up in being a career person. Alex was dismayed and resentful that his gifts were not well received. Projecting is a setup for frustration and disappointment; it may be that our expectations cannot be met.

Here is an example of two people who seem to get what they want, at least for a while. Zack and Maria fell in love and were inseparable for years. They were completely symbiotic, synchronous in everything they wanted—a small house in the country, a dog, jobs they could do at home, and frequent vacations to sunny spots around the world. They found unity, as only people with a good dose of padma can do. Their relationship became everything to them. They formed an alliance in which they conformed to each other's wishes with an unspoken agreement that differences would be avoided. Hardly existing as individuals, for some time they cocooned in the world they had created together. They thought their relationship would last forever.

However, the glow faded, and Zack began to feel trapped. His karma-family urges to seek adventure, to be on the road again—he had been a photographer for *National Geographic*—became greater than his desire to be with Maria. Even though she could have accommodated prolonged absences on his part, this development was too threatening for Maria. She became clinging; Zack became defensive. When the mutual projection fell apart, their partnership ended in bitterness.

When partners in a relationship maintain boundaries, there is less projection and more space to see each other's mix of colors. When we see the full spectrum of energies at play between us, we can accommodate differences without being threatened by them. A buddha person can give a lot of space to a ratna person; a karma can help make things happen for a buddha; a vajra can calm the emotional turbulence of a padma; a ratna can nurture a karma; a padma can bring ease in communication to a vajra. Every relationship involves a subtle dance between surrendering to the other person's energy and staying in touch with our own.

DIFFERENT DOMINANT QUALITIES

Each combination of energies has the potential for both rigid polarity and complementary merging. People who have different dominant energies often complement each other beautifully and enrich the relationship with their different qualities. But contrast can also heighten their confused patterns. If one person is an entrenched blue while the other person is unremittingly red, the lack of flexibility results in reactivity, which creates a chain reaction: the more aloof the vajra, the more clinging the padma. These dynamics create further distance. To hold their ground, both parties solidify who they are as a defense against the other person's energy. They become polarized through resistance. When they are able to open and merge, however, their styles balance each other out.

Here is an example of a long-term relationship in which the emotional patterns have become clear and the partners have been able to work with them consciously. Justin and Rose derive a great deal of satisfaction and enjoyment from their professional lives. When they have free time, difficulties arise, because they have different ideas of fun. Rose likes to do things together: socialize, travel, take a vacation, go out to dinner—a padma world. Justin likes to spend time alone, engaged in one of his many learning projects. At the beginning of their relationship, Rose kept trying to tell Justin he didn't have to work so hard. Then she finally realized that this was his way of having fun—a vajra way.

Every weekend Justin and Rose face the same question: how are they going to spend their time? Usually they just fall into their habitual patterns and end up resenting each other. He resents her for pressuring him to interact, and she resents him for not interacting. They fall into the trap of blame. Sometimes when the dynamic becomes extreme, they exit to their mask energies: Justin dulls out into buddha, and Rose becomes a busy karma. His dullness only exacerbates her busyness and vice versa.

When Rose and Justin harmonize, it is usually because they have planned their time so that both are able to do what they want. She allows him space to study, and he accepts her invitation to socialize. He might tell her what he is reading so they can talk about it together. At other times she appreciates his spaciousness, which allows her plenty of room to be herself.

When Rose and Justin became more conscious of their exchange, their relationship improved. But addressing the problems inherent in their energy dynamic depended on their being able to surrender their own demands to some extent. Then their particular mix of energies allowed them to open each other up. They could be who they are, together. Healthy merging is a blend of brilliant colors, not one color blotting out another. (We will explore this process further in chapter 17.)

My daughter, Chandra, and I used to clash around the morning ritual of getting up and out the door. I like to move quickly—putting away dishes, getting breakfast together, making lunches. But trying to hurry her in the morning only created tension. Picture organized and efficient karma mom bumping up against indulgent and comfort-oriented ratna daughter. Chandra, in her ten-year-old wisdom, came up with the solution: she set her alarm early enough so she could get up and snuggle with her cat, read, and take her time getting dressed.

The same dynamic came up after school. Chandra took an exceptionally long time writing assignments. It put our whole family under pressure to make sure she got her papers in on time. Again, I kept trying to speed her up. It was only after a parent-teacher meeting that we saw what was going on. Chandra loved to create imaginative, highly descriptive stories, which took a lot of time. In acknowledging her creative process, we were all finally able to appreciate Chandra's integrity and allow her to be who she was.

SAME DOMINANT QUALITIES

People in partnership who have the same dominant qualities can also run into challenges. Trying to communicate through just one energy style can result in a dysfunctional relationship. Other energies are necessary. These are often available through the enhancement energies. For example, Linda and Bruce both had a lot of fiery padma energy. They were always running hot and cold together, solidifying the push-pull of passion and aggression into an unworkable energy dynamic. Since they were not in touch with other colors in themselves, they enlisted a counselor with a cool vajra perspective to point out the natural ebb and flow in their relationship. She was able to identify the other colors in their relationship that could make it more workable and less extreme. Linda and Bruce finally began to focus on their work. Karma energy was able to ventilate their situation and soothe its fiery padma energy. Karma helped them reconnect at the place where each of them had something to offer. It helped them open to a bigger world.

For predominantly padma people, it's particularly helpful to make friends with their energy in a light-handed way and cultivate the energies of other families. Other energies—particularly vajra and karma—provide some grounding and stability. Underlying padma relationships is an acute sense of distrust. How can we trust anyone who flips and turns with the fluidity that this energy displays? One day she says she wants to be with you; the next day she is entertaining the possibility of another relationship. Yet however torturous it may look from the outside, a padma-dominated relationship can be enjoyable. Pain and pleasure combine in an intoxicating drink. If padma partners can appreciate their mix of energies and work with the padma element so that it does not become too extreme, their relationship can flourish. And if our lives seem rather flat compared to those of our padma friends, we could even find ourselves envying them.

Here is an example of two people with karma energy. Sybil and Annette are successful, energetic women working in the same organization. Sybil is the director; Annette is a department head working under her. Between the two of them, they often become speedy in trying to fulfill the demands of their roles. Both like to be competent and responsible.

When Sybil and Annette are operating in their own domains, their relationship is smooth. But when Sybil makes decisions that affect Annette's department without consulting her, Annette becomes infuriated. Sybil, on the other hand, doesn't see it that way. She thinks that since she is the director, everything is her domain. As you can imagine, tension between these two ladies can mount. When two karma people are racing around each other, sparks fly just from the friction of the speed. The situation often escalates into confrontation. The tension created by the energy can affect everyone.

To resolve their differences, Sybil and Annette realized that they had to relate to each other consciously, making their relationship a priority. They asked for a facilitator to open communication between them. They made a deliberate effort to connect with each other in social situations, bringing in more padma energy. Each of them began to appreciate the tremendous work the other was doing instead of feeling threatened by it. The fact that Sybil and Annette both also have strong padma energy makes communication natural for them. Padma and ratna are good antidotes to excessive vajra and karma energy.

CONSCIOUS RELATIONSHIPS

Good relationships don't just happen. In making them workable, we often need to arouse intention and expend effort. This is conscious relationship. Such relationships do not occur only in the intimate realm—though surely that realm holds the potential for maximum opening. Conscious relationships can also be found between people in any work or social situation.

Sometimes one person—perhaps the one reading this book—is more ready than the other to have a conscious relationship. Beginning a conscious relationship with someone who is unwilling to explore this mode of relating is like trying to dance with a dead weight.

In such a case it will be hard to have clarity about the relationship. For example, Jessica was aware of many of the energy dynamics between herself and her husband, but every time she wanted to talk about them, he would become defensive. She knew that they needed to seek therapy to get through their difficulties, but her husband refused to do this. The relationship became blocked.

In a healthy relationship we share our sanity. If there is too much closed energy, the relationship will bring both people down. Continuing may not seem worthwhile. One person might come to feel that her individual development has a higher priority than the relationship. It takes two to tango. If someone's energy is repressed—either because of the relationship or independently of it—the partnership will remain unworkable or at least unsatisfying. No tango.

Here is an example of a relationship that went through a long process before becoming conscious. Early in their working partnership, the relationship between Charles (vajra) and Aaron (karma) became heated because they had such different ways of doing things. Charles wanted to spend considerable time planning their joint business; Aaron just wanted to get in there and test different possibilities. At first they tried giving each other feedback, but the "feedback" was often thinly disguised aggression. The more they attempted to hash out their differences, the more the situation intensified. They blamed each other for being at odds. Both became reactive and defensive, further entrenched in their individual styles. Nothing was working.

Then Aaron had a mild heart attack and took a leave of absence. The two found their relationship helped by the space that this afforded. They began to see the positive aspects of their differences: Charles had vision, and Aaron had organizational skills. But they couldn't see this until there was some space in the relationship. Then, because they were able to find their own ground and feel confident in themselves—more open—each was able to appreciate the other. They could recognize the complementary aspects of each other's styles. Separating gave them the spaciousness to merge and the ability to enter into a conscious relationship.

Sometimes verbal communication (or physical in the case of intimate relationships) is what is most needed to make a relationship conscious. Timing is crucial. We have to soften ourselves before trying to communicate. It helps to generate openness and maitri. Especially when there has been considerable negativity in a relationship, it is helpful to set some time aside to talk about it. You and your partner can decide together that on Thursday evening or Saturday morning each week, you will sit together for an hour and just discuss your relationship. Even your willingness to meet in this way is a sign of openness. The awareness exercise at the end of this chapter provides a useful technique, appreciative inquiry. It can also be helpful to consult a trained professional facilitator or therapist.

Five energies work has great potential to help us make a relationship conscious. If we can really see another person's colors, we can appreciate his display. If both partners in a relationship are able to do this, each person's energy has its own dancing ground. There is room for our song and dance, his song and dance, and the play of colors between us. The abundance of our own mandala is enriched by intermingling consciously with the mandala of another.

EXERCISE: APPRECIATIVE INQUIRY

This exercise, which arouses sanity and appreciation for each participant in a conscious relationship, is adapted from one used in organizational development and therapeutic work. It can be done with two people or with a group.

One person interviews another and takes notes. When answering the questions, contemplate which energies are present. For example, someone might answer the first question by saying, "When I practiced meditation for three months" (buddha), "When I focused on writing a book" (vajra), and so forth. The first person starts by asking the second person the following questions:

1. What are the times in your life when you have felt the best?
2. What are the external conditions that made that possible?
3. What qualities in you made that possible?
4. What are the times in your relationship when you have felt the best? (This could be any relationship with any person, including the interviewer.)
5. What are the conditions or circumstances that made that possible?
6. What qualities do you see in the other person made that possible?
7. What aspirations do you have for the relationship, separately and together? How would you like the relationship to be in three to five years? What would you like your contribution to be toward making that happen?

When one person has finished, switch roles. Then talk with each other about this process or bring your answers back to the group.

After the exercise you might feel that the negative aspects of the relationship have not been dealt with. Trust the exercise and ride the sense of positive outlook that has been created. When you focus on the positive, you see your sanity clearly, and neurosis falls away. If issues remain, you could do another session of appreciative inquiry around them later.

11

Living in the Mandala

Four hundred of us were living together that spring in a quaint old hotel, all studying Buddhism and practicing meditation. This was overwhelming for the hotel switchboard operator, more accustomed to handling guests who did not know one another. Come the cocktail hour, she was inundated as never before with calls from one room to the next. And she made mistakes, connecting this room to this rather than this room to that. She soon realized that it didn't seem to matter whom she plugged into whom. We all seemed to have something to say to one another!

This is an illustration of mandala principle—the inherent interconnectedness of the five energies. In essence a mandala is an energetic field encompassing the totality, the big picture. A mandala is a map: the flatlands of spacious energy, the peaks of intellect, the lush valleys of abundance, and so forth. The map is also moving, like a weather map on TV. Connecting to the mandala provides a sense of universality, a larger vision and greater perspective. It could be the mandala of our family or the weather or our body or our workplace. In Tibetan Buddhist art, mandalas depict whole cosmologies resplendent with iconographic detail. The four cardinal directions are sometimes represented by deities in the vajra, ratna, padma, and karma families, while in the middle of the mandala is a deity representing the spaciousness of buddha-family energy.

Whereas the solid, concrete world creates boundaries, the energetic world creates connections. The perspective of mandala is less egocentric than our ordinary perspective because we are not the constant reference point. Visualizing ourselves as the center of our own mandala requires recognizing that we are multifaceted and many-dimensional. The mandala puts our perspective in a larger context. It liberates us from our little way of perceiving things. Seeing the big picture takes a big mind.

INTERCONNECTEDNESS AND TOTALITY

The totality of mandala perspective has to do with our inner psychological world as well as the outer phenomenal world. The landscape of thoughts and emotions is our inner mandala; the external world is the outer mandala. There is a constant play between the two. In any given moment they are informing each other.

Our sense perceptions form a bridge between the inner and outer mandalas. They are our antennae, feeding data from the outer environment to our inner world of thoughts and emotions. How we see the world depends on our internal reality. (More on sense perceptions in chapter 14.) For instance, when I first moved to Nova Scotia, wow, how I hated the weather. All those rainy days and all that cold wind! But as I made friends, established my private practice, and furnished our home, soon the weather, that same cold wind, didn't seem so bad. It was really rather refreshing.

It can be truly amazing how inner and outer worlds influence each other. One stormy Nova Scotia night, my husband, daughter, and I all awoke from wild dreams. From the basic energy of the external agitation, we each produced our own agitated story line in a dream. The energy was there; we provided our own data.

The way the five energies play themselves out in the natural world is a mandala. The moisture of rain (vajra), the heat of the sun (padma), and the rich nutrients of the earth (ratna) make plants grow. The rain falls into streams and rivers and flows to the ocean, where it mixes with air and evaporates to become clouds (karma). Then it turns into rain again. The rain falls, the sun shines, and the earth nourishes without bias. Space (buddha) accommodates it all, also without bias. It is a total energetic system in which each distinctive element contributes its vital quality to the big picture.

Our body is also a mandala. Our skeleton gives us our structure; we could think of it as having a vajra quality. The soft flesh and skin all over the body are ratna. The blood pulsing through our veins, lubricating and connecting, is padma. Our muscles, which generate activity and function, are the karma element. The cerebrospinal fluid, which is at the core of our very being, is experienced as the spacious, all-accommodating quality of buddha.

Likewise, in a family unit each person plays a role within the whole. Let's take a look at the Williamson family around dinnertime. Each of them provides a unique quality that keeps the family energies balanced and interactive.

Thomas, the father, came home from work at five-thirty and immediately went to fix the leaky faucet in the bathroom. He tends to be project-oriented around the house but can also enjoy a good, rough game of football with his son, Vincent. This is karma energy.

Rita, the mother, has spent the day making the rounds of the antique stores she frequents. The house is full of her previous acquisitions. When her daughter, Angelica, came home from school, Rita helped her with a costume for the school play. Then she fixed a scrumptious dinner. Rita has lots of friends and loves to play hostess. She constantly nourishes and supports her family. This is a ratna/padma type of person. Though her house contains many antiques (ratna), they are all arranged tastefully (padma). She loves having her friends drop in on her spontaneously (padma) but also enjoys preparing an elaborate dinner for them (ratna).

Although Vincent, like his father, tends to be active, he has a quiet side, too. He has been studying in his room since he came home from school. He likes to read and think. At dinner he will no doubt pose penetrating questions about life for his parents to answer. He thinks he will major in science at college. He has some strong vajra qualities.

Angelica is full of fun and play, with many friends and all sorts of ways to entertain herself. For her, life is brimming with excitement, and she is always trying new things. She likes clowning around and brings a sense of delight to the family. She is thinking of becoming an actress. She is a strong padma element in this family.

You can also see your life as a mandala composed of family, intimate relationships, work, and spiritual path. The energy of each field affects the others. You might find that your work is teaching you something about yourself that gives you insight into your relationships; your job might be informed by a particular energy that arises from your spiritual discipline. Something you learn from your relationship with your family might influence your spiritual path. In the mandala the five energies are continuously informed and enriched—or contaminated—by one another.

At one point my husband and I looked at the mandala of our relationship by doing the appreciative inquiry exercise at the end of the last chapter. We had been aware that padma energy was often missing in our marriage: intimate time always seemed superseded by work, community, or family needs. To remedy this, we consciously brought padma energy in by carving out time to have quiet dinners together, exchange massages, and make love. Then when we looked at the mandala of our lives, we realized that ratna—home, hearth, food, family time—was the most absent element. Cooking together, nurturing plants, making bright, colorful curtains, paying attention to our indoor lighting, and making more family time enriched our environment and lives considerably.

One person who worked with a different color every day said, "The contrasts are what I was very aware of—being dipped in fresh color and completely forgetting the experience of the day before. Each was so rich in itself. The flavors of all, in the end, seemed vital to be able to access. Each without the others seemed so locked in, too something—cool, sharp, sappy, sentimental, overblown, anxious, dulled, flat."

CYCLES OF ENERGY

The sense of inclusiveness or totality of a mandala can be seen over time. For instance, all the families are represented in the developmental stages of a child. A baby in the womb is in buddha energy. An infant primarily concerned about his comfort is ratna. When he starts to be inquisitive about his world and connect with it, he enters the padma family. As a toddler, he finds his physicality to explore with karma energy. School brings out the vajra in him, to study and gain knowledge. By age eight he is fully formed, with all his colors flying.

Another sequence of energies is the mandala of a day. For example, observing my natural rhythms, I've found that in the morning I tend to be clear and focused. So I use mornings for activities that involve overview and planning as well as precision and detail. This is vajra energy. Morning was the best time to write this book, for instance, so I tried not to schedule other commitments before noon while I was writing it. In the afternoons and evenings, I am more likely to be interested in reaching out to people. This padma energy is useful for relating with clients or having meetings. Sometimes I find it calming to do the accounts at night. This activity has a clear, cool vajra quality. Occasionally I declare a "domestic day" and go at household chores and errands in a karma way. Seeing these patterns has become a determining factor in planning what I do each day. It's a very practical example of how knowledge of the five energies can be helpful.

The interconnectedness of the five energies sets up a certain dynamic. One energy triggers another. If the dynamic results in the solidification of each energy, a negative cycle results. For instance, the ignorance or immobility of buddha, when it starts to stir, can turn

into vajra's anger and criticism; this could lead to a desire to dominate the situation and become ratna's pride. Next could be the consuming desire of padma's passion, which is wanting to possess.
Finally, wanting to protect the possession would be karma's paranoia.

To illustrate: More than once I've been in an audience listening
to music or watching dance with great passion and longing as I connect with the performance. But when the show goes on a little too
long, I start to criticize the performers and become angry. Finally I
tune out. Thus I've gone through passion, aggression, and ignorance
(padma, vajra, and buddha), with each energy being triggered by the
one before.

Another way the energies affect one another is that intensified
vajra becomes karma; intensified padma becomes ratna; and any family intensified becomes buddha. To elaborate, if vajra's feeling right
becomes too solid, it moves into karma's need to take action. If a
padma person feels rejected, he will cling to the person he still loves.
However, that could very likely lead to a sense of ratna's poverty.

A positive cycle might look like this: the openness and all-
accommodating space of buddha become the inquisitiveness and understanding quality of vajra, which lead to the richness and possibility
of ratna, which become the appreciation of detail and refinement of
padma, which lead to the action of karma. This is a cycle for the creation of anything—a work of art, a business meeting, a society. It can
happen very quickly, almost in a flash, or it can build more slowly.

NATURAL INTELLIGENCE

Our energies possess an inherent intelligence. For instance, staying
with one kind of energy for too long makes it fixated, which feels
draining because it throws us out of balance. When I feel as if I'm
depleting one particular color on the palette—by sitting at the computer too long, for example—I switch energies by changing activities
or resting. I might want to get out of my head (vajra) and get into

my body with karma activity or padma/ratna sensuality. Then I feel energized. Altering rhythms is refreshing.

When we are sensitive to energy, we can make intelligent choices about what energies we need at a given time or what energies we most want to cultivate altogether. I saw that a friend of mine was listening to the play of energies in her life when she told me the following. She had undergone major surgery, which necessitated her being literally "opened up" to the cold, antiseptic vajra/karma hospital environment. She discovered that what she longed for during the months of her healing was warmth and nurturing. She became padma flirtatious. Because of her illness, her old house no longer met her own or her family's needs; she found a new one in which she was able to nurture herself with ratna comfort. Bringing in the warm energies helped her to heal. Then the brilliance of her vajra intellect and the more discriminating side of her padma energy returned.

Likewise, an energy that has been ignored for too long will erupt in some way. When we reach the end of our tether with busyness or stress, for example, we crave the spacious, restful quality of buddha energy, which our culture tends to ignore. By undertaking a contemplative practice like meditation, we find more balance. When we become aware that we are composed of fluctuating energies, we can draw from the whole palette of possibilities to get what we need. Being aware of the full potential of colors and how they mix expands our vistas.

THE MANDALA AT WORK: ORGANIZATIONS AND GROUPS

The work of Peter Senge and others in organizational development has introduced the idea of systems thinking. This work applies the mandala principle in that it regards a system as the complexity of dynamic structure rather than as isolated events or people. To be effective, an organizational structure needs to contain all five energies: vajra provides vision and clarity; ratna enriches the situation with a sense of possibility for expanding and is very resourceful; padma lubricates the situation to enhance good communication and is a pleasure to have around; karma is dependable in becoming organized and getting the job done; buddha is totally amenable to whatever is happening and thus provides good support. When the energies are not in balance or some of the energies are missing, the whole organization can quickly fall into a negative spin. When all five energies are present, in various combinations within people, the group or organization is more likely to function smoothly. There is tremendous potential to dance with energy creatively. Here are some examples.

Jack, who very consciously works with the energies, is director of a nonprofit organization that relies heavily on volunteer labor. Those volunteers who have been in the organization for a long time feel that they know how things should be done. Because they know one another well, they have strong feelings about one another, both positive and negative. The ensuing displays of emotion and strong opinions sometimes jam up the operation. Jack might know exactly what to do in a given situation, but more often than not, he must first deal with an emotional storm, and it takes tremendous patience to hold his clarity while doing so.

In this case Jack's strong vajra quality (dominant) with a dose of buddha (enhancement) makes him an excellent choice as director. He can allow a lot of space for events to unfold. At the same time he can see a situation's many facets and what is needed to move it forward. He can cut through the discursiveness of multiple opinions and get to the main point. Though he listens to what is being said, he does not buy into the emotional dramas. People like working with him because he accommodates them and their ideas. He leads by including.

Because Jack knows about the five energies, he can hire people based on their energy styles. Matching a person to a job is a subtle art. One must know what kind of energy is needed to perform the job, be able to recognize someone's style, and be aware of the possible energy dynamics among coworkers. Jack knows that a team has to have different colors. With knowledge and practice, Jack can mix the colors in his organization skillfully.

In one political situation I know of, the incumbent leader was a vajra/ratna type—clear vision rich in possibility—but his interpersonal skills were lacking. Another party leader (karma) saw what was needed to make things happen. However, these two men could not communicate very well. Their relationship was at an impasse until a third man (padma) came along who was able to facilitate communication. A strong display of four styles simultaneously enabled things to move forward.

A director of an organization came to his job with an inspired vision (vajra) and sense of possibility (ratna), but he lacked the skills to bring things to earth, make things happen (karma). As well, he had strong buddha tendencies when he became overwhelmed. His staff, who had worked together for years, gave it some time but found themselves waiting for direction. Because none came, the organization's energy became diffuse (buddha). Operating with only three colors, like a car running on three cylinders, the organization could function, but not well. What was lacking was more communication between the director and his staff about action plans and timelines (padma and karma). A personable and hardworking person was hired as manager in hopes that she would move things forward.

Balancing the energies at our workplace is another way of bringing in mandala perspective. If we consider that most of us spend a major part of our day at work, it seems vital to find that balance. Most office workers are stuck in vajra and karma; factory workers have too much karma; and so forth. How can we balance this out? My son, Julian, worked for a while with kids at risk at an agency in Oakland, California. He was the only white person in the office. When Al Green came on the radio, everyone would just get up from their desks and boogie down for five minutes, then return to work. Yes! In my work with organizations, I encourage people to institute a "just being" break (buddha: people sitting quietly for a few minutes) and a "just moving" break (padma/karma: people dancing together for five or ten minutes). The shift in energy could be quite refreshing and inspire greater productivity.

Being aware of mandala principle in a group is the same as working as a team. A team forms when people drop their personal agendas and offer what they have to the whole. When the energies of each team member are acknowledged and properly used, the relationship among the elements of the mandala is lubricated and each energy family communicates clearly with the others. Knowing how the five energy families interrelate facilitates this communication. As well, when there is trust in the mandalic connections, each element is strengthened as team members continue to move forward by setting their personal agendas aside.

In therapeutic work, too, we can see how mandala principle operates. For example, open-format process-oriented group work allows plenty of room for individuals to be themselves. The dynamics of people's energies show up in the immediacy of the moment and in a constant play of relationships. Vajra people often voice strong opinions when there is confusion, or they become critical of others, sometimes displaying aggression. Ratnas are full of need; they never seem to get enough time to air their issues. Padma people tend to be the most emotional and often pick up on the emotions of the others. Karmas may not talk that much and yet become impatient if very little seems to be happening. Buddha people hardly talk at all and need to be invited to participate.

Group process is a wonderful way to see mandala in action. By creating an open space with no agenda or system to follow, you can allow whatever arises to play itself out. Everyone becomes a mirror for everyone else. For instance, padmas may get very upset with the cool, emotionless opinions of vajra people. Conversely vajras and karmas could get impatient with the emoting of padmas and ratnas. Buddhas will withdraw even more if the energy of the atmosphere becomes overwhelming.

Family systems theory, a systemic approach to therapy, is based on the understanding that an individual's psychological dilemma can be perpetuated by family relationships. The perceived client is continually influenced by the dynamics of the family. Let's take Ben, who's fourteen and has a lot of karma energy. His family, like many others, is dealing with alcoholism. After Ben displayed aggressive behavior in school, therapy was recommended, but it was only somewhat helpful. Ben's behavior did not change all that much, nor did his basic attitude of defensiveness and aggression.

As often happens, the person identified as the therapeutic client is merely the focal point of a much larger problem. He has become the site of the eruption, like the escape valve on a pressure cooker. But treating the client in isolation can resolve the family dynamics to only a certain extent. At some point the therapist decided that Ben's whole family needed to be included in the process. After several sessions with the family, the dynamics surrounding Ben come to light.

Ben's father, a vajra/ratna type, has become an alcoholic in middle age after losing his job, yet neither he nor his family deals with this fact openly. About once a week he drinks too much and is abusive toward others in the family, particularly Ben, who just isn't good enough in his father's eyes. Although Ben's mother is a karma type who is usually pretty busy, she is very buddha around her husband's behavior: she chooses to ignore what she can and put up with what she can't rather than confront him. When he's sober, Ben's father is loving and cares for his family. In any case, he is least aggressive toward Ben's older sister, who has many friends and after-school activities and thus is not around very much. Her energy is padma. She also chooses to ignore what is going on.

However, as the father's alcoholism becomes more of an issue, each person's habitual energy pattern becomes intensified. Ben's mother gets busier, his sister stays away from home more to be with friends, and Ben acts out aggressively. Therefore, to identify the confluence of forces creating the dysfunctional situation, the mandala of the whole family needs to be considered. The interconnectedness of the energy dynamics in toto must be examined and worked with. Working with Ben alone will never get very far.

CONFUSION AND SANITY IN THE MANDALA

The mandala is sometimes chaotic and confusing and sometimes clear and orderly. When the mandala is confusing, it is because we are seeing only our version of events; when it is clear, it is because we are seeing the play of the five energies as they are.

When we are closed, we become fixated, convincing ourselves that our view is solid. We are always projecting and then coloring our world with our interpretation. We create realms. Any argument, however trivial, is essentially a projection: one person solidifies events into his version, and another solidifies them into hers. Solid views bumping up against each other can escalate into confusion and even warfare.

When we are open, we can rise above our projections and see all the energies inherent in a given situation. Our mind is more spacious. Not only are we more likely to see another person's view, we are also likely to tune in to the fleeting, impermanent, transparent quality of energies at play. We can dance with the energy of the present moment.

At a business meeting someone with ratna energy might just want to stay in the comfort zone of the status quo. A karma type might be pushing for innovation. Awareness of the tendencies and energy patterns of each family will give us the wisdom to see that there is room to accommodate both styles. We'll be able to realize that keeping the stability of the status quo in some areas can actually enrich and support new ideas and that new ideas bring fresh energy. The patterns begin to make sense. There is order, intelligence in the seeming chaos. Recognizing the potential for order, we are less likely to be overwhelmed by the chaos.

To penetrate confusion, we need to look at the combination of someone's tendencies and the particulars of his situation. It is all too easy to blame someone; looking at other factors widens the perspective. It is important to consider the many causes and conditions that contribute to a difficult situation. Rather than immediately jumping to the conclusion that someone has an unworkable personality, we could simply say that he is not the best choice for that situation: a loner might work less well as a director than as a consultant, for example. Looking at the situation, we could ask, Is it set up for failure or success?

For instance, Raquel was trying to be an equal member of a team despite the fact that she was geographically quite removed from the other members of the team. As they bonded and moved forward, Raquel continually felt left out and undermined. On the one hand her input was highly valued, but on the other hand her attempts to remain included began to be resented. Lack of trust and tension arose. The situation was set up for failure until management redefined Raquel's position as being that of a visiting consultant. Other factors can also come into play: differences in private lives (one work partner's having a strong family life and the other person's being single), differences in economic status, racial differences, language and cultural barriers, and so forth.

Here is another example. As the director of a company, Curtis has a lot of forward-moving energy (karma) and likes to get things done. He often charges ahead with projects, frustrated with his coworkers, who seem slow and inefficient in the wake of his activity. He chooses instead to relate to his immediate superior, the president, an old friend. This dynamic was already causing resentment when, backed by his superior, Curtis made the major decision to move the company to another town—a decision that affected not only the employees but their families as well. Several people in leadership positions were outraged that their vision for the company (vajra) had not been considered. Parents had concerns about their families and homes (ratna). Single people in relationships experienced separation anxiety (padma). As opinions hardened and emotions escalated, factions formed: people aligned with like-minded others and blamed those with dissimilar views. The two sides could not see each other's viewpoint at all. What they did have in common was that everyone blamed Curtis.

In this situation clarity could only come about if everyone opened to the full display of energy. Making Curtis the scapegoat would have focused on the energy of one person rather than acknowledging the whole picture. Many meetings were held, and people were allowed to hear all aspects of the issue. Eventually everyone agreed that although the decision itself was a good one, something that had to happen (visionary vajra), the way it was handled lacked skill (neurotic karma). The more personal ratna and padma concerns could also have been avoided if the decision had been made with more communication and forethought. In the final analysis, no one was really to blame; once the energy dynamic had been set up as it was, conflict was inevitable. With awareness of the play of energies, however, the conflict could have been avoided.

In these ways, by becoming aware of the interconnectedness of the five energies in ourselves and in those with whom we work and live, we open to the play of the mandala.

EXERCISES: THE MANDALA AT WORK OR HOME

This series of exercises could be done by a group of people who are working or living together. How long the exercises take will depend on the size of the group. A larger group could divide into subgroups if needed. With one or more groups of ten people, the exercises could take about four hours with a lunch break. In general it is best to have an outside facilitator. The exercises are designed to:

- Help participants bring the whole person into the workplace or living situation
- Create an opportunity for participants to see one another more fully
- Permit more effective teamwork, as the full potential of each person is brought out
- Enable participants to communicate on more levels, with more colors

- Help participants see the energetic makeup of the organization and environment
- Permit greater cohesion based on mutual respect and teamwork
- Enable participants to create a more harmoniously functioning organization or living situation

Personal Energy Map

1. The group facilitator describes the essential characteristic of each energy in both closed and open manifestations. He or she asks, "Where in your life, in what kinds of situations, do you experience each energy?" Group members note their responses on five file cards.

2. Group members then place their cards in a personal mandala, as in the exercise at the end of chapter 9. People can briefly share with the group what thoughts and feelings have arisen in doing the exercise. With a large group this will take too much time, so the exercise could be self-reflective.

Just-Being Break

Group members sit quietly for three to five minutes, paying attention to their breathing.

Group Energy Map

In an open space create a map (mandala) with an area for buddha in the middle and vajra, ratna, padma, and karma in each of the four directions (as in the exercise at the end of chapter 9). In the following exercise people might find themselves straddling two energies. If so, work with two.

1. Group members go and sit in the area that represents the energy that they feel is most familiar, home base, whether it's an energy in which they get stuck or one in which they can shine. When all

members have positioned themselves, they talk among themselves about why they are there.

2. Next, group members move to the area that represents the energy where they feel their personal power or intelligence, where they shine. (Some members may stay where they are.)

3. Then group members go to the area that represents the energy where they experience their power at work. (Again, some members may stay where they are.)

4. Group members note with whom they communicate most often. People can say how they experience the energy of the relationship and what aspirations they have for it.

End with a group discussion of the experience. Then take a lunch break.

Just-Moving Break

Put on some music and have ten minutes of guided or free-form movement. Anything goes.

Group Energy in Project Management

This exercise involves working with a case study. It is most effective when the situation is current and has some charge to it. Sitting in a circle, do the following:

1. One person gives a brief description of the situation.
2. Everyone then entertains the following questions:
   What energies do you bring to the situation? Stuck? Open?
   How could you contribute more? Shine more?
   What do you need from others to make that happen?

End with a group discussion of the experience. What happened? What did you learn?

PART THREE

AWAKENING INTUITIVE AND EMOTIONAL INTELLIGENCE

12

Training in Nowness

You now have the big picture of the five energies and how they make up the mandala. This section of the book presents additional tools, guidelines, and suggestions for bringing the five energies into your life. Sharpening your tools will take some work; using them will take some practice. Stop reading from time to time and do the exercises at the end of the chapters. They will give you firsthand experience with the material presented here.

BECOMING AWARE OF HABITUAL PATTERNS

We have already worked with our psychophysical barometer, becoming more sensitized to energy and particularly to our open and closed states of mind. We are now going to deepen our understanding of this tool by using it to see how our habitual patterns arise throughout the day. Seeing our patterns involves learning not just how we are in the moment but how we are over time. Looking at our deeply ingrained habitual patterns—as we did when learning to recognize our style—highlights certain behavioral tendencies that occur over and over again. We see how thoughts, emotions, and actions build from flickers of mind to emotional explosions to acting out. We see how we are perpetually preoccupied with certain tenacious thoughts. We might notice an itch-scratch response to our experience—how we automatically react to whatever arises. For example, if our experience presents what we want, we feel good; if it doesn't, we try to push it away.

Simply by learning to observe yourself, you can begin to notice when you feel touchy and easily irritated. You can witness yourself undergoing upheavals that manifest as anxiety or angry outbursts. With patience and awareness, you can learn to see your emotional reactivity to situations, how you create your own personalized soap opera or, conversely, how you keep emotional energy locked in your body. If you can notice when you feel stuck, claustrophobic, and dense, you'll be able to determine when your energy is bound and fixed. Again, look at your breathing. Is it relaxed or held? The next step is to notice whether you feel chronically entrenched with your particular energy pattern or only occasionally so. Do you feel total paralysis or just mildly dissatisfied some of the time? Or perhaps in spite of looking well adjusted and successful, you just don't feel connected to your life. There's no sense of play. All these are ways of learning to see when your energy is stuck.

At particularly stressful times—the death of a loved one, unemployment, divorce, or catastrophic illness—our energy becomes heightened and our style exaggerated. It's as if we believe that intensifying the energy of our habitual patterns will make the situation less groundless. We become a caricature of ourselves. Looking back on any intense period in your life can be revealing. For example, reflecting on a time in my life when I felt confused, I see now that I had tried to find clarity through analyzing and had become obsessed with trying to figure it all out (vajra). Because I wanted emotional support, I had talked to my friends (padma) so much that they got tired of hearing from me. Feeling that I must do something about my confusion, I had become perpetually preoccupied with the situation (karma). These are the three energies that are most active for me when I am intensified.

ATTENTIVENESS AND AWARENESS

In order to see our habitual patterns, we need to cultivate the ability to be self-aware. Self-awareness requires attending to the present moment by observing what is happening. We can train ourselves to do this. Attentiveness—also called mindfulness—and awareness are the basic components of sitting meditation practice. Through this practice we can stabilize our minds, which, in turn, brings mental clarity and an inherent strength.

As well, sitting meditation acts like a lightning rod. It grounds overly volatile energy in the simplicity of just being here. Attentiveness and awareness are the most basic tools for working with both the inner mandala (thoughts and emotions) and the outer mandala (people, places, situations). I invite you to work with these two tools on your own in sitting meditation. The easiest way to do this is to find someone to instruct you and a group of people with whom to practice. Appendix C, "Places to Practice Meditation and Maitri," contains a list of helpful resources.

Attentiveness

Attentiveness is the ability to bring our attention to the present moment. Being in the present moment—the only moment—stabilizes the mind. When we are attentive to the present moment, we are not jumping from one sense perception to another, nor are we engrossed in our thoughts or emotions. Instead, we are attentive to what we are doing in the moment that we are doing it—like brushing our teeth. A stabilized mind brings us present into the now. It brings our mind and body together in the precision of moment-to-moment experience. Mindfulness synchronizes mind and body in one-pointed attention. We can remind ourselves to be mindful by bringing our attention back to our breath whenever it occurs to us.

Attentiveness is taking a simple attitude toward our activity. This is easier when we slow down, do less. When we reduce our mental speed, we can synchronize thought and action. We can see what we are doing and be aware that we are doing it. Physical activity that demands staying in the moment is a good way to train ourselves in attentiveness. We can be attentive in any activity—eating, washing dishes, driving, housecleaning. If we stay focused on the movement and physical sensations without mental wandering, we are synchronizing mind and body. The result is a sense of well-being.

Mindlessness is doing one thing while thinking about something else, dividing our attention. Mindlessness takes us away from what is happening. If our mind slips away or we try to do two things at once, mind and body are split. When we do things habitually without being present—like spacing out, daydreaming, fixating, or obsessing—we are mindless. Mindlessness is lack of awareness, not knowing what is going on.

Sometimes mindlessness can be frustrating, as when driving and missing a turn, or it can be dangerous. A friend was riding a horse that bolted. Try as she might to slow him down, he kept picking up speed. What she did not realize, as those of us watching did, was that in the confusion caused by the horse's sudden burst of energy, her riding crop was hanging loosely and gently tapping his flank, urging him on: "Go faster!" It wasn't until she heard "Drop the crop!" that she was able to rein the horse in. Being mindful can save your life.

Being mindful actually disrupts our habitual patterns and punctures our incessant need to solidify ourselves. It keeps us from wandering off into our projections. Mindfully returning to the present moment protects us when we knowingly ignore what is good for us, what keeps us sane. Being where we are brings a tremendous sense of relief, because we can settle into the simplicity of the moment.

When we are mindless, we become energetically unbalanced—as when we push too hard and get strung out, manic, or exhausted. Mindfulness synchronizes us so we are energetically balanced. It enables us to experience the energies with more sanity. If we have a glass of muddy water—our usual active and discursive mind—any color we add will just make it muddier. If we allow the mud to settle, then we have clear, pure water. Any color we add will look vibrant and brilliant.

Awareness

Attentiveness develops precision; awareness develops panoramic vision. Settling the mind by attending to the present moment brings with it a certain relaxation. Relaxation creates the space in which to see clearly what is happening in the moment. As the mind settles and becomes more focused, it naturally expands, and we become more aware of what is around us but without getting lost in it. Most people report that after a session of sitting quietly, they find the world to be much more vivid and alive.

Awareness gives us the freedom to receive the total environment and interact with it attentively. It allows us to develop appreciation for where we are. When we are open in this way, we aren't thrown off by circumstances, because we have the stability of mindfulness. With stillness of mind (attentiveness), the activity of mind can be seen more clearly (awareness).

There is a growing body of evidence that meditation reduces stress. It helps us to learn to "go with the flow." My experience is that when I bring my mind to stillness and hold my seat, whatever happens, I will not get upset. On the other hand, if I become speedy and caught up in the circumstances of a situation, flying all over the place, I react negatively to the slightest inconvenience.

Awareness is an intelligence that is direct, present in every moment. It is not about collecting insights that will eventually change our behavior. It is a kind of understanding, a knowingness, that is based on the energetic experience of synchronized heart and mind in the continuity of the present moment. We see clearly in the moment and know what to do. This quality is heightened when being in the moment is a life-and-death matter—as when we're skiing, rock climbing, kayaking. These sports are exhilarating because there is no choice but to synchronize mind and body.

INSIGHT

Awareness awakens insight, our natural intelligence. Insight arises when our mind is relaxed. It is the ability to relate directly without concept to the patterns of energy in ourselves, in others, and around us. When we let go of concepts about our experience, then instead of resorting to a tired formula like "I'm having a bad day," we can be in each moment with a fresh perspective.

However, if we hold on to our insight as a reference point, we become fixed once more in a conceptual, analytical understanding of how we think things are. We use it to build a story line. Unlike a story line, which is tight and fixed, insight is loose and open to interpretation. It is fresh mind. When we are relating to the energy of each moment, there is nothing to hold on to. Insight that arises also passes. We learn to let it go.

Awareness allows us to discriminate between the insight of direct experience and habitual layers of conceptual filter. It allows us to begin to notice how we create confusion and claustrophobia when we see the world through our filter of how it "should" be instead of opening to how it is. When we relax our defensive mode (also called "me") and open to how things are, we become more aware of our environment and can harmonize with it. Then we feel at ease dancing with the colors.

ATTENTIVENESS, AWARENESS, AND RIDING THE ENERGY OF THE MOMENT

Attentiveness and awareness come together when there are both active thoughts and intelligent stillness. The stillness helps us to see more clearly the deep waters of our inner mandala and the energetic play of the outer mandala. We can relax in the buoyancy of the ocean and also feel the movement of the waves.

Bringing attentiveness and awareness together is like flying a kite: You hold the string firmly (attentiveness), and then the kite can fly high in the sky (awareness). If you do not hold the string, the kite dances wildly in the sky. If you hold the string too tightly, the kite will never reach the sky. Holding the string just right while feeling the kite's movement is joining attentiveness and awareness.

This is how Erin finds attentiveness and awareness helpful in looking at her habitual patterns. Her energy dynamic is that she has a lot of ideas (vajra) and a strong sense of wanting to put them into action (karma). She gets into a solidified sense of "I'm right" and "Let's do it." When she's on her own, this is no problem. In working with others, however, she tends to move too fast. When she takes the time to settle her mind and allows herself to be sensitive to what is going on—doing exercises like the ones at the end of this chapter—she can catch herself speeding. Then she slows down and becomes aware of the bigger mandala of which she is a part. Sometimes she still doesn't catch herself in time. Either she's been too assertive, or her speed has caused confusion. In any case, she continues to practice catching herself.

One of the high points of my dancing days was doing contact improvisation, a dance form based on being in continual contact with a partner. Through the entire dance, you are alert (attentive) to every movement impulse of your partner and conscious (aware) of the space you are in and the people who are watching. Movements— lifts, falls, spins, catches, leaps—all follow one another in spontaneous response to the flow of energy between the two people. It is an exhilarating way of riding energy.

I don't dance that much anymore. Now I ride horses. Maggie was the first horse I fell in love with. Settled in the saddle, my hands on the reins, my legs at Maggie's sides, I am attentive to every nuance of energetic shift between us. When we are "on," we are one. When she puts her ears back and is about to shy or hesitates before a jump, I give her a responsive gesture to support her. We are connected, communicating. I am also aware of the arena—the sunlight coming in the open door; my husband, John, on Loco; the tractor in the corner; my reflection in the mirror as we pass it; the voice of my instructor, Andy, guiding my ride through a thick Polish accent. I'm attentive; I'm aware. And I'm flying like the wind. I'm riding the energy of the moment.

LETTING GO OF "ME"

When we practice being self-aware, we work on letting go of "me," our self-centered strategy for controlling our world. When we relax into the space that allows us to see our habitual ways of operating and reacting, they become less convincing.

For example, I had spent months dwelling on what I thought was the solution to the communication problems I was having with my colleagues: an infrastructure that would allow clearer lines of communication. I was frustrated and impatient with the others for not seeing it my way. When I realized how convinced I had become that my way was the only way, I relaxed and had a good laugh. Whatever I had cooked up had no steam left in it. My clarity was intact, in that I still thought an infrastructure would be helpful, but I no longer felt angry or assertive.

Feeling bad or stuck often provides the impetus to begin working with ourselves. When we feel wretched, we want relief. Expanding our awareness can also be an impetus because it plugs us into our intrinsic sanity, which is characterized by openness, clarity, and compassion. We long to cultivate those qualities. We might feel calmer yet energized. We can do more without getting stressed. We see that we don't have to struggle with ourselves so much. Cultivating sanity in ourselves and recognizing it in others is a catalyst for this journey.

Usually we're so busy, so preoccupied, that we are unaware of our thoughts, emotions, and actions. But when we can cut through the speed of accumulating thoughts, they lose their thrust toward solidification. Our habits become less compulsive and automatic. We no longer strongly identify with thoughts and emotions because with mindfulness part of our awareness remains detached. This observing self—which we cultivate by being mindful and aware—is more objective about who we really are, what we're saying and doing. We can watch ourselves get angry or depressed, we can hear our outburst, we can recognize what our frustration is truly about. We can catch the process in the act, interrupt the operation, undermine our complex mind. Dismantling the architecture of ego like this is called letting go.

I hit upon the idea of using a common event to train myself to work with habitual reaction. I decided to watch myself sneeze and discovered that if I followed the arising of the sensations of a sneeze with alertness about the whole process, the impulse to sneeze was not followed by the automatic explosion. I found this telling: merely being attentive and curious transformed my sneezing experience. Since sneezing is rather innocuous, with no real charge, observing myself was relatively easy. Watching myself getting angry is much more difficult. Try experimenting with both.

When we start poking holes in the way we are used to operating, when we take our life apart by looking at it closely, we can become very self-conscious. We don't quite know who we are or how to act. I call this "contemplative constipation." It is a necessary phase in the process of self-discovery. We'll feel uncertain, with many questions and doubts. Sometimes we'll feel embarrassed, frustrated, hopeless, or disappointed. At the same time, we will also begin to be more relaxed, open, and inspired. We begin to glimpse islands of clarity, moments of intrinsic sanity. This inspires us to continue our self-exploration. When I connect to my intrinsic sanity, it feels like basking in the sun on a hot summer day without the slightest inkling of what the clouds were about.

EXERCISES: ATTENTIVENESS AND AWARENESS

Sit on a cushion on the floor with your legs crossed or in a chair with the soles of your feet on the floor, in an upright posture. First, just take note of how you are: tired? speedy? emotional? Acknowledge where you are without judgment. Then decide how long you want to do this exercise, but do it for at least ten minutes.

Begin by turning your focus to your breathing. Breathe easily. Allow your breath to go in and out without trying to change it in any way. Let the breath be the object of your meditation, your sole reference point. As your breathing is happening in your body, you may also be more aware of the sensations of your body, the breath going in and out.

Let your gaze be relaxed and slightly lowered so you don't get distracted. Bring your body, breath, and mind to quiet and stillness as much as possible. You are just sitting and breathing, with your mind being with your sitting and breathing.

You will be more successful in doing this if you arouse strong motivation: "I am sitting here with the sole intention of stabilizing my mind." The more often you can do this, or the longer, the more settled and calmer you will feel.

Choose one activity during your day and aspire to do that and only that. It could be morning exercises, washing the dishes, driving to work. Be attentive to every movement. Watch to see how and when your mind wanders.

Wander aimlessly inside your house or out in the garden or along the sidewalk. Be aware of everything that is going on without getting involved in anything.

You could also try this for fun. Take a teaspoon full of water and walk around with it, not spilling a drop. At the same time be aware of everything around you. This is bringing attentiveness and awareness together.

13

Embracing Who We Are

We have looked at different ways, different tools, to bring the energies into our lives and make them useful to us. When energy becomes heightened, however, we need a very powerful tool—the tool of unconditional loving-kindness, maitri (mentioned in the first chapter), which allows us to be who we are unreservedly. Maitri provides a catalyst for us to enter the process of transmutation, a fundamental change in energy. Working together, maitri and transmutation enable us to experience the inseparability of confusion and sanity.

The process of transmuting neurosis into sanity, as we have seen in the energy descriptions, is the ultimate challenge of working with the energies. In essence, each energy is neutral and teeters on a razor's edge of going toward wisdom or falling into confusion. When we stay on that razor's edge, essential change comes about by our recognizing the inseparability of neurosis and sanity, the ultimate wisdom of energy work. We go beyond aligning with sanity (the sun) as opposed to confusion (the clouds); we embrace all aspects of who we are. When our sun and our clouds come together, we are a rainbow. We embody our wisdom.

THE ANATOMY OF EMOTIONAL BUILDUP

An emotion is the peak experience of a collection of thoughts. Emotions begin with the smallest flicker of a thought. As thoughts pile upon thoughts with increasing speed, they solidify and intensify into an emotion: thought-thought-thought-thought, emotion. Then we "feel" the thought as a psychophysical experience. Not all emotions are particularly neurotic. Some emotions that we feel very fully—the deep sadness of mourning the death of a loved one, the joy of giving birth—merely reflect our genuine heart of tenderness. Any emotion can become fixated, though, and that stuckness is what we are addressing in this section.

When we experience an emotion neurotically, our mental chitchat cleverly builds a solid narrative to justify how we feel. We call this the story line. Since we tend to view our thoughts as totally believable, in turn, we identify heavily with our emotions. Our emotion has an object or a reference point ("I'm angry at so and so") and justification for it ("because he did such and such"). Our thoughts feed and focus the feelings. Our story lines rekindle the emotions. We find ourselves entrenched in the cycle of emotional intensity called a realm. (To review the realms, refer to chapter 3.)

Because we identify with our emotional story lines so strongly, it is hard to relinquish them. They justify us, confirm us. "I want to be angry. I want to be jealous. I want to be morose. This is my truth!" We feel loyal to our version of reality. We hang on tight, as if by letting go of our emotions, we would dismantle our whole known world. If I am pining over a lost love, giving up that melancholy means that the whole drama of my affair is gone, which means that a part of me is gone as well.

When our emotions become too painful, our overwhelming desire is to get rid of them. We don't want to feel their intensity. We deal with not wanting to feel them in different ways. Some of us suppress our anger or jealousy or passion by denying that we are feeling it. We suppress because we think emotions are shameful or too overwhelming to experience. We might even think that we have let go of the emotion. We can pretend to do this, but unless we've felt the feeling fully first, we're probably fooling ourselves. Our anger or passion is still down there, ready to pop out at any moment.

Or we might be intensely angry, but we are so caught up in our story line that we are not even aware that we're feeling emotional. We latch onto our solid version of reality as a defense against feeling the emotion. Someone might even say, "You seem awfully angry," and we simply deny it, snapping "I'm not angry." Or someone might say, "It looks as if you're falling in love with him." "Oh, no, he's just a friend," we reply. For jealousy it could be, "Why are you always putting him down and being annoyed with him?" "I'm not. He just needs some feedback." Suppressing feelings leads to mental and physical illness. Emotions get locked in our bodies.

Another strategy for trying to get rid of emotions is to act them out. We explode or otherwise indulge our feelings. Like suppression, this is just another way of not relating to the energy. Acting out comes from the panic that our anger—or passion or jealousy—is too much to bear. Although screaming at someone or threatening to kill ourselves might feel rewarding, in fact this approach perpetuates emotional entanglement. It only creates more confusion and intensifies our emotions.

Whether our style is to dump the emotions on ourselves by bottling them up or to dump them on someone else by acting them out, there is an alternative to trying to get rid of them. The best way to work with our heightened states of energy is to befriend them. Difficult as they are to work with, intensified emotions and the projections that arise from them can be turned to our advantage. They radiate loud and clear what is going on. If we can step back and look at our projections and the drama we have created, it is possible to see them as energy—the play of color, quality, and texture. Enlisting maitri—unconditional loving-kindness—gives us a tool for transmuting confusion into sanity. This is the ultimate challenge of working with the energies.

CULTIVATING LOVING-KINDNESS

First, let's take a closer look at the tool of maitri. We introduced it in the first chapter as the ability to love ourselves, embrace who we are. Maitri is having an unconditional friendliness toward ourselves. Accepting ourselves as we are, in both our sanity and our confusion, is the key to opening our heart. It allows us to be in the present moment just as it is, without trying to cling to it or push it away. Accepting ourselves fully is what stops our struggle. It allows us to appreciate ourselves and our world despite the obstacles. Only when we love ourselves in this unconditional way can we also love others. Only when we love ourselves can we lovable. Maitri has a soft quality that is open, kind, relaxed, warm, and inclusive. It allows us to be who we are and let all our colors shine. We breathe easily.

Some people seem to exude loving-kindness. They radiate a sense of well-being and warmth. Although we tend to think of these people as padma or ratna types, maitri can be experienced in all five colors. The energy of maitri can be equally, but more subtly, present in buddha, vajra, or karma people. Maitri gives us an ease in being who we are, whatever our energy: a clear and precise vajra, a generous and accommodating ratna, a compassionate and loving padma, an all-accomplishing karma, or a calm and spacious buddha.

Maitri is lacking when we feel bad about ourselves. When we are judging ourselves or reacting to someone else's judgment about us, we are more neurotic. We raise our defenses, project onto others, and close into a realm. It may seem impossible to think of ourselves as lovable when heavy negativity is coming toward us. At such times it is natural to build a defensive wall to justify what we did or said. Our openness and friendliness toward ourselves disappear.

Deeply rooted self-hatred is likely to be internalized by children who come from a background of neglect, abuse, or criticism. For instance, Ann was neglected by her parents and sexually abused by a male relative when she was very young. Her only source of unconditional love was her grandmother, whom she seldom saw. By the time

I met her as a therapy client, love in Ann's life was "long gone." Her self-hatred was intense. Convinced that she was fat and ugly, this petite woman was locked into a prolonged cycle of bingeing and purging. The cycle was driven by a harsh, critical "warden" who kept her cycling through the realms, trying to find some ground. None of them worked. These realms were real for Ann; she had names for herself in each of them.

Even without a critical environment, it is easy to feel bad about ourselves when we bounce from one constricted state of mind to the next. We can feel bad regardless of our style: we are too critical and sharp (vajra), we are too needy and greedy (ratna), we are too obsessive and grasping (padma), we are too controlling (karma), or (the hardest to see) we are too much in denial (buddha).

A common reaction when maitri is missing is to seek love outside ourselves. Feeling warm, open spaciousness coming from someone else can be a lifeline. Some of us find unconditional love in our intimate relationships (lovers and friends); others find it with therapists or teachers. Ultimately the idea is to internalize it, to cultivate maitri within ourselves. Nevertheless, it is much easier to experience maitri when the environment is infused with it. Sometimes all it takes to kindle self-love is a smile or a big hug from someone else.

I knew that Ann needed to be surrounded by maitri. Her grandmother had rocked her and sung her lullabies. I did the same. Although sometimes she would soften and cry, it was very hard for her to internalize maitri. I realized that just working with maitri was not sufficient; we also needed to work with transmutation. Ann's story will continue later in this chapter.

There are many ways to experience loving-kindness. Sometimes words don't do it for me. I want to be touched. Getting a good, sensuous massage softens my rough edges, and I feel warm and integrated. Maitri comes through the hands. Healers know this very well. Sometimes music can soften. Albioni's Adagio or Bach's "Air on a G String" can bring tears to my eyes. Music and massage combined are a magical maitri-infusing combination.

ASPECTS OF MAITRI

Maitri has several aspects, each of which sharpens our understanding of how it works. This is the intelligence of maitri. These aspects are often—but not always—experienced in the following order:

1. Maitri has an element of familiarity. This involves being acquainted with our habitual patterns. They don't throw us off. They feel like old friends. We know that we have a tendency in a certain direction: too bossy (karma), too quiet (buddha), too critical (vajra).

2. Maitri involves accommodation. Having made friends with our habitual tendencies, we no longer hate ourselves for them. When we see the intensity of our closed energy—when we get angry at someone, for example—we no longer try to avoid what's happening. We allow it to be. We accommodate our neurosis and so expand our palette of acceptable energy states.

3. Letting ourselves be infused by the warm quality of maitri relaxes us. It allows us to be gentle and kind toward ourselves. Our pain is still there, but instead of avoiding it, we care for it as we would care for an open wound.

4. Working with maitri enables us to develop bravery, which means that we can touch our vulnerable, raw spots and still stay open. Intensely emotional situations demand this kind of bravery.

5. Our life experiences are workable. When we encounter an unwanted circumstance, we don't give up. Rather than contract and close, we open to the situation. We see it not as a crisis but as an opportunity. Maitri allows a sense of workability in our lives.

6. This last aspect of maitri includes all the others, in that the quality of friendliness toward ourselves is unconditional. Having maitri means that we are friendly toward all aspects of our experience, sane or confused. It means that we are friendly with our constricted views, our small mind, the facets of ourselves that we like the least. We can love ourselves without reserve, with zero stipulations.

TRANSMUTATION IN FIVE COLORS

Along with attentiveness and awareness, maitri makes transmutation possible. It is the key, the catalyst, the synergist to fundamental change in ourselves. The basic premise of transmutation is that sanity and neurosis are not separate. Rather, they are different qualities of one indivisible, essential nature. There is wisdom in the most heightened moments of confusion. Being familiar with the energies and how the wisdom of the energy is born from the inseparability of confusion and sanity is helpful in seeing how transmutation works. What follows are some short illustrative sketches for each family. Remember that with the many colors that could be present, transmuting intensified energy may not be this simple or straightforward in real life.

Embedded in *vajra* anger is vajra's wisdom, an ability to see things clearly. A vajra person transmutes her energy when she sees that she can be clear or "right" without imposing it on anyone else. Her sharp intelligence that led to anger transmutes into seeing the world with mirrorlike clarity, vajra's wisdom.

When a *ratna* person makes friends with his sense of inadequacy—feeling needy and greedy—he is able to relax into feeling enriched by and appreciative of his world. He transmutes his energy by seeing that the richness of the world is also in himself. He feels a sense of equanimity, ratna's wisdom.

When a *padma* person stops manipulating situations to avoid what is painful and attract what is pleasurable, she transmutes being both critical and clinging into discriminating awareness. Her ability to connect to the world from an intimate, feeling level allows her to be acutely sensitive to subtle differences in the inner and outer environments, a discriminating awareness, padma's wisdom.

The driven busyness of a *karma,* fed by paranoia and jealousy, relaxes when his passion to do is not fed by a sense of feeling incompetent. He transmutes his competitiveness when he realizes he can accomplish whatever he wants with ease in a timely, appropriate way, the all-accomplishing wisdom of karma.

A *buddha* person's immobility and ignoring, her confused quality, when relaxed, transmutes into a sense of spaciousness that begins to see everything as OK. She transmutes her energy by realizing that since there is nothing to be upset about, there is no reason to withdraw. She can embody an all-encompassing spaciousness, buddha's wisdom.

THE PROCESS OF TRANSMUTATION

When we apply the six aspects of maitri to an intensified emotion, we engage in a transformative process. We move from letting go to letting be. The pith instruction is to stay with the primary emotion we're feeling. Making friends with the essential nature of the emotion that binds us offers the possibility of liberating it. Both the story line and the quality of the basic energy may differ, but the process remains the same. We may even find another emotion underneath the one we're working with.

Here is how I have worked with the aspects of maitri in transmuting my emotions. Although it may look like a neatly packaged process, going through it can be confusing and overwhelming. As I have mentioned, I am often carried away by jealousy. With attentiveness and awareness, however, I've begun to be able to recognize jealousy as it arises, before it becomes full-blown. I see that it can be triggered simply by hearing of a rival's accomplishment or seeing an object of my jealousy walk into the room. I know how jealousy feels in my body (familiarity). Now when I feel it happening, instead of reacting, I let it be (accommodation). Sometimes my jealousy is very intense. Becoming aware of my breathing and feeling an open place in my heart takes the edge off my emotional intensity, allows me to get in touch with warmth and relaxation (warmth). I sometimes feel scared by the situation and my reaction to it. However, even though I feel shaky, raw, and vulnerable, I stay with it, neither acting it out nor suppressing it (bravery). Jealousy is now quite familiar to me. Whereas in the past I would turn my jealousy into a big drama, now

I can embrace it without feeling overwhelmed (workability). The unconditional aspect of maitri means that whatever I am going through is OK. I don't have to judge myself—good or bad—if I am having an emotional day. At times jealousy has been the green meanie; now it's more often the green wake-up light (unconditional).

My friend Tim was prone to anger. Because we were living together, I became involved as he worked with his anger. Sometimes I was able to bring maitri into the situation when he was not. Tim's angry outbursts would sneak up on him. They seemed to "come out of the blue." He could be banging his hand through a door or shouting at me before he knew what he was doing. The first step was the hardest for him: realizing that he was angry (familiarity). I was frightened by his outbursts but also knew it was important for his anger to come out into the open so that it could be acknowledged. I tried not to overreact, giving him the space to let it happen (accommodation and bravery). After acknowledging his anger, he tried to stay with the intensity. Often he wanted to be alone to let himself feel the quality of his anger. He could feel it as constriction in his body, primarily in his jaw, throat, and chest (accommodation). He stopped struggling with it, stopped trying to push it away. At first that is about as far as we could go. We would just drop it.

As he became more familiar with and accommodating of his anger, Tim began to feel more relaxed. It was no longer such a big deal (warmth and workability). The fact that it took years for him to develop an unconditional attitude toward himself is not unusual. The transformative process of maitri is something we practice over and over again.

Since transmutation is about going into our emotional pain rather than trying to get out of it, external support can be very helpful. Ultimately, however, we have to do it for ourselves. Remember Ann from earlier in this chapter? At one point an encounter with the family member who had abused her sent her into deep depression for four months. Since she chose not to seek therapy, it was not until almost a year later that I heard the full story. Although she was still functional in a mechanical way in her job as a pediatric nurse, emotionally she had bottomed out. During that time the only thing between Ann and suicide was the fact that she didn't know who would take care of her children.

Then there was a shift. Ann read a book on primal scream and began to remember what we had discussed: staying with the emotion rather than pushing it away, relaxing and being kind to herself. On her own she stayed with the process of transmutation for about three months: "I hurt in every way, at every level possible, every minute, no matter what else was going on. But it was OK. I didn't need to do anything about it. I didn't talk to anyone. The biggest thing that I discovered was that my parents couldn't love me. It was simply a fact, like the table is brown. I can't remember how the hurting stopped. Since then things are better." The eating disorder that had plagued her since her teen years disappeared. "It's as if the food stuff happened to someone else. Now when I'm hungry, I eat. Before hunger was a trophy [in that it meant she had conquered her desire for food]." "I no longer have thoughts of suicide. Life gets crazy at times, but nothing goes on that I can't handle." Most important, she said, "I feel." She could experience her energy without closing into a realm.

Working this way with our emotions even once, we have more confidence in our ability to do it again. As Trungpa Rinpoche said, "When you make friends with your craziness, you are not crazy anymore." Ann was quite triumphant that she was able to make friends with herself. Now she feels that she has more energy in everything she does and more patience with her children as well as everyone else. Her role at the hospital also began to change. Now she is the person to call when there is difficulty with a young patient, because she works with the children so gently. Coming out of her own pain, she has discovered compassion. Working with transmutation inspires us to take on the challenge of working with other people. As Ann puts it, "I just take my time with whatever needs to be done."

PITFALLS AND POSSIBILITIES

Story Line

As we have seen in discussing the anatomy of emotional buildup, our story line heightens the intensity of the emotion. So the story line can be a pitfall. When I get caught in a story line, I seem to do things that perpetuate my emotional charge. For example, I talk to my friends until they no longer want to hear about my turmoil. I analyze the situation by writing reams of thoughts. Splitting up with a boyfriend many years ago, I wrote ninety pages in a journal, trying to figure it all out—what he had said and my response, what I had said and his response, what I could have done differently. It did not make me feel any better. Sometimes, however, it can be useful to let our story line have full rein. We can even exaggerate it to see what fictitious beliefs or unrealistic expectations the stuck energy is breeding.

Creative Expression

One antidote to the story-line pitfall is working with creative expression. Creative expression takes us out of our heads into the immediacy of hands-on work. It allows us to stay with the emotion at an energetic level without acting it out or denying it. Sometimes I write about the emotional experience as it is happening, as in stream-of-consciousness writing or spontaneous poetry. Rather than analyze, I stay with my experience by briefly touching pen to paper. When I feel that I am starting to analyze, as in the journalizing mentioned above, I return to what is more immediate—my feelings.

Dancing has been a primary way I have expressed my emotions. When my mother died, I spent a year creating a dance called "Elegy." I would move and cry, move and cry. That is the way I mourned her passing and went through the many stages of transformation in relation to her death. Sometimes I felt as if I were indulging in the pain, dwelling in my sorrow. However, I was also aware of the change in my emotional state as I grounded it in an activity. The dance ended on a note of joy.

Indulging, Suppressing, or Staying with the Energy

How can we tell whether we are indulging, suppressing, or staying with the energy? We can begin to discriminate among these strategies by becoming aware of how they make us feel. Indulging by acting out emotions feels explosive. Suppressing by bottling them up feels tight and frozen. Staying with energy in an open, inquisitive way feels intense, too, but it also feels wholesome, spontaneous, and appropriate. When I indulge or suppress my emotions, I feel exhausted. I am acting impulsively, without synchronization. When I stay with my emotion without acting out or suppressing, it feels genuine and spacious. Then I feel energized.

Exiting as Antidote

Sometimes using an antidotal energy is an alternative to transmuting our confusion. Whereas habitual exiting to another energy as a mask is neurotic, exiting as a conscious choice can be an expression of maitri. For example, when we are caught in a confusing emotion, it can be very helpful to exit to karma. Getting physical with sports, dancing, or a brisk walk has the power to cut through emotions fast. Being the padma kind of guy he is, my son often gets caught in heartache. We can talk for hours on the phone about it—long-distance maitri. Aside from encouraging him to lean into his pain, accepting it, I push him to play soccer (karma), another passion of his, or to get back to work (karma) or to spread his desire for relationship to his many friends (less fixated padma).

Fear

Fear is another pitfall. When we lose control of our car on an icy road, fear is an appropriate response. However, in many other cases our fear is an inappropriate projection: we see the rope on the ground as a snake. It is because we feel threatened that we become emotional. Fear underlies all emotions. For example, someone gets credit for a job you feel you have done. Underneath your jealousy and anger might be the fear that your job is at risk. Your world is threatened. Or let's say that your neighbor has just had a huge party to which you were not invited. You feel poverty-stricken and friend-less. Underneath these feelings lies the fear that you are in fact an unlovable person. The fear underneath emotion can immobilize you. However, in becoming aware of its presence, you can learn to contact the underlying fear. You can then examine the core feelings and beliefs that have given it power. Then it is possible to be with fear without being overwhelmed by it.

BRILLIANT SANITY

When we use maitri as a tool, we find that we could either laugh or cry. At the point when we laugh or cry, the struggle is over. There is a sense of breakthrough. We have broken through our sense of con-stricted self. We have touched our heart.

After a long and tumultuous relationship, my son reconnected with his sense of humor. He had called in distress, and after a short talk, I had left him with, "Stay with the intensity and make friends with it." Later he got on the phone and in his inimitable way said, "Did you clock me? Three hours. How's that for turnaround time?" He was back, being himself, full of humor. Another time, in an E-mail, "She waffles . . . consistently . . . and I laugh, . . . and it feels so good to laugh . . . something in a laugh that is more than just pleasure but a kind of essential acceptance. . . ."

Maitri is a matter of the heart. The heart is what experiences the fullness of the energies. When we let our experience be exactly as it is, we can see the intelligence, the brilliance, in our perceptions. When we embrace the energies in ourselves, we begin to trust the brilliance of our intrinsic sanity; it begins to shine. Our brilliant sanity—the purity of our energy—reveals itself. Maitri is the key that opens the door to our brilliant sanity. We feel allegiance to our sanity. As my son says, "It feels better to be happy."

EXERCISE: CULTIVATING MAITRI AND TRANSMUTING

If you are not used to working with intensified energy, do this exercise in a group or with someone who can provide a compassionate presence. Work with the primary emotions associated with each family—hot or cold anger; puffed-up pride or self-pitying poverty; clinging, craving passion; competitive jealousy; or denial, ignorance. You could also work with other emotional feelings such as grief or guilt. As you do the exercise, remember one or more of the six aspects of maitri as described in this chapter: familiarity, accommodation, warmth, bravery, workability, and unconditionality.

1. *Sitting:* Sit for about ten minutes with a sense of just being. When you feel your mind wander, come back to your breath. Allow your mind to settle. Then close your eyes.

2. *Intensifying:* Touch something painful that's happened to you recently, around which you have an emotional charge. If another person is involved, imagine his face as the object of your emotion: if you are angry, be angry at him. Feel the emotional energy in your body. Use your breathing to heighten it. Let the story lines feed and justify the emotion. Let your whole body feel the energy: feel the muscles tighten, particularly in your face, hands, arms, and upper body. Move into a posture that expresses your emotion. If sounds want to come out, let them. Keep intensifying. Intensify until you experience the energy as just energy, unbiased toward open or closed.

3. *Transmuting:* While focusing on your breathing, let the pain and confusion penetrate your heart. It could feel like a wound. Stay with that. Then with a deep breath, flood your heart with maitri: a

soft, warm, melting energy. You might begin to get tears in your eyes or even cry. Breathe gently in and out. Feel your body relax. Feel the energy radiating out from your heart through your whole body. Let your body be infused with the warm, fluid energy and let go of the constricted energy completely. Feel the power of the energy in your body. Do this long enough to experience the strength, brilliance, and intelligence of your energy.

4. *Radiating brilliant sanity:* Again picture the person who was the object of your emotion. Radiate brilliant sanity; radiate maitri toward him. Drop your story line about him. Feel compassion toward him.

5. *Sitting:* Return to just sitting and breathing at the end of this exercise. You could do this for ten more minutes.

Sometimes once you have worked with one emotion, another one surfaces—like the anger that might arise from working with passion. At a later time you could work with that.

On-the-Spot Practice. Here is a quick version for when you find yourself in the heat of an emotion:

1. Become aware that you are experiencing an emotion; acknowledge it.
2. Stay with the intensity.
3. Take a deep breath to bring yourself into the present moment. Melt. Let yourself be infused with maitri.

14

Becoming Sensational

Our first understanding of the energies is most often a psychological one: we want to know who we are, how our personality manifests, how we relate to others. Indeed, in the last chapter we saw how our brilliance, our wisdom, is embedded in our psychological makeup. Yet, as we have seen in the description of the families, the energies pervade all aspects of our existence: both the inner mandala of thoughts and emotions (psychology) and the outer mandala of phenomena. The energies connect us to the phenomenal world at an elemental level. We experience the outer mandala by extending the antennae of our sense perceptions—seeing, hearing, smelling, tasting, touching.

It may sound simple, and we might assume that we do it all the time, but when we truly connect to our sense perceptions, it is a sensational experience. They may lead us into a world we only thought we knew. Sense perceptions invite us into the present moment, where we naturally expand. They give us a reading on the outer mandala; they invite us to join the play of energies. As well, they ground and nurture us, often dissolving our emotional fixations. They can even be an antidote to emotional upheaval.

There are two ways we expand our awareness of sense perceptions. The first way is to see the connection between each sense perception and its particular family; the second is simply to become more attuned in general to opening to them. The simple exercises at the end of the chapter are helpful for enhancing our ability to tune in to the world and come to our senses.

THE FIVE ENERGIES THROUGH SENSE PERCEPTIONS

Each of the five energies is associated with one or more sense perceptions. Though there are different schools of thought on these associations, the following are the ones that work best for me: seeing for vajra; smelling, tasting, and the sensation of touching for ratna; hearing for padma; and touching as connection for karma. No particular sense perception is associated with buddha.

Sense perceptions can give us a distinct sense of who we are. We experience ourselves differently when seeing, when being touched, when smelling, when tasting. In each case certain aspects of our world open up. For instance, when we focus intently on seeing—as in taking a photograph or working at a computer—we relate to the external world in a vajra way. When we fully focus on smelling and tasting—as while cooking and eating—we enter a ratna world. When we hear what someone is saying by the tone of her voice and pick up on the emotion rather than her words, we tune in to padma energy. When we swing an ax, kick a ball, or put our foot on the gas pedal— touch something in a functional way—we are in karma family.

In relating our sense perceptions to the five families, we can learn to be very precise. For example, in looking at a photograph, we might say, "Oh, that's very ratna." But in using our eyes to have the experience, we are in fact experiencing a vajra take on ratna. A truer ratna experience would involve smelling and touching—like getting a sensuous massage with patchouli oil. How does that differ from looking at a ratna photograph? By cultivating precision with our sense perceptions and allowing ourselves experiences in all the families, we can widen our palate of permissible energies. If we allow ourselves to experience our sense perceptions fully in the present moment, we will see how we literally become different people as our perceptions change.

Most often we use several sense perceptions in a given moment. Chefs know that a meal must not only taste good (ratna) but also be pleasing to the eye and communicate that it is pleasurable (padma). At the same time, vajra and karma elements are involved: an overview of the meal is necessary as it is cooking (vajra), and activity is required throughout the process (karma).

An affinity to one sense perception might tell us something about our mix of colors. As a choreographer, I delighted in the body's ability to express itself in many shapes and patterns as it moves through space. The work of the visual artist M. C. Escher also entered my choreography. I took his themes and turned them into movement. I am also finely tuned in to how objects are arranged in space—the relationship of large and small objects, colors, and textures—and how open, spacious spaces and contained, closed spaces are created. Even in taking up macramé, I saw the instructional diagrams as movement patterns. I enjoy moving furniture, plants, lamps, and art objects around my house to get different effects. When I go into other people's homes, I mentally redesign them to my liking. This is working with the sense perception of sight, associated with vajra. Since it arises from my aesthetic sensibility, it is mixed with padma. Because visual perception creates a subject-object relationship, there is always a distance involved in this perception. With padma mixed in, it is warmer and more inviting.

Though, as a professional dancer, I was very involved with my body, I did not pay much attention to its sensations. I moved to the demands of the choreography. In the middle of my dance career, I discovered massage and became a massage therapist. Now that I am more aware of it, there are times when I crave being touched. In ratna, touch has everything to do with the sensations of our body. We can experience this by having someone touch us or by developing our inner awareness of our body. If there is no one around to give us a massage, sitting meditation—or any other contemplative discipline—is a way of touching ourselves from the inside. Ratna is also associated with smelling and tasting. We all know how satisfying and nurturing it is to smell and eat good food. Thus the three sense perceptions associated with ratna are visceral. We experience them deep within our body.

Padma is associated with hearing. In this case what we mean by "hearing" is a sense of picking up the vibrations of a person or situation. This perception helps us to intuitively sense the energetic—or emotional—landscape. We talked about this in chapters 2 and 3. This larger understanding of hearing as vibration is the perception most akin to working with the energetic aspect of who we are. We experience vibrations in the outer world—in particular as sounds and music—that strongly affect our inner landscape. Music of any kind, particularly love songs or romantic pieces, stirs our emotions. This quality is probably what we like most about listening to music. Music can change our mood quite dramatically. Speech—in poetry, politics, or theatrical performances—can have the same effect.

Touch is associated with karma. In this case touch has to do with making a connection to an object or to a movement—like picking up a cup or swinging a baseball bat or your leg. In this context our understanding of touch is functional rather than sensational. As a dancer, I know the connecting quality of touch well, as when my muscles engage to make a movement happen. Athletes also work with connective touch. Karma touch is about moving to connect with the world.

Buddha energy has no particular way to connect to the world through a sense perception. However, because it is open to receiving all of the senses, it acts like a switchboard, a receptor, for the other families.

Now that we have seen how our senses open us to different experiences, we will look at how to cultivate these experiences by training our sense perceptions.

COMING TO OUR SENSES

There are times in our lives when we suspend our agenda and really take in what is around us—walking in the forest, sitting quietly by the fire, listening to music, or looking out a train window. We come back to simply being here in the moment without editing it. Just as being present is the first step in becoming aware of our thoughts and emotions, so it is also vital to truly opening our sense perceptions.

It is inherently good and wholesome to let ourselves be. When we are in the present moment without the conceptual filter of "me," the environment feels nourishing because we let it touch us rather than trying to control or manipulate it to please us. We can have a gentle relationship with it—like sitting in a park on a sunny day with the breeze catching the leaves of the birch trees, the children playing by the lake, and the bikers going by. We aren't holding on to our territory. We're most likely to experience this sense of letting be when we are on vacation. Away from our busy workaday world, we relax and open.

When we are fully present, we are receptive. We can receive the phenomenal world around us. Opening to sense perceptions, we become a sensate being. Then when we see a color, we see it with our whole being. Being fully present, when we look, we actually see; when we listen, we hear; when we smell and taste, we savor it; when we touch, we truly feel. Plugging our sense perceptions into the phenomenal world is the key to directly contacting reality beyond concept. In this place we are able to experience the play of energies nakedly.

Most often, however, our mind fluctuates between experiencing directly and experiencing through the defense of a conceptual filter. We paper over our experiences with expectations, projections, and story lines. Unable to stay with the present moment, we are not open to our world. Our mental activity clouds up our channels and twists the perceptions we receive, producing a dull, distorted view. As we have seen, fear and anxiety underlie much of this habitual distortion.

They keep us from openly receiving the world. We hardly let an experience take place before we feel compelled to name it, as if we must solidify it by putting it in a little box with a label and tucking it away. Then we are no longer having the experience; in fact, we are avoiding it. Simple preoccupation with our thoughts and emotions can also keep us from seeing what is around us. For example, driving down a California highway on a beautiful day, I ran out of gas. I had been so absorbed in my thoughts that I didn't see the stunning landscape around me, nor did I see that I was low on gas.

Plugging directly into the world around us with our sense perceptions can be a practical way to live. We may find that by receiving support from the environment in this way—wherever we may be—we will be less dependent on our personal relationships for nourishment. Learning how to open our sense perceptions fully gives us a way of letting the world become our dancing partner at any time, any place. Opening to our senses can also calm our emotional upheavals. There's a reason we might storm out of the house when we're upset: just moving through space, being in the body, letting ourselves be nourished by our sense perceptions, is calming. We can consciously tune in to the outer mandala as a way of shifting our inner state.

INVITING MAGIC

Nowness and openness are the keys to experiencing things as they are. When we tune in to the world by fully experiencing our sense perceptions, we experience it as powerful and magical. For example, once when I was leading a workshop on sense perceptions, smelling a stick of cinnamon took me to another world. Though it's a spice I have used all my life, smelling it in that moment transported me to the sensuous environment of an Ottoman harem. Very ratna indeed.

The positive aspects of the five styles of energy become more vivid when we open our sense perceptions. However magical, though, working with the senses is also a down-to-earth experience. Different spaces, environments, or situations have different psychological effects on us. We can't necessarily change those effects, but we can stop resisting them by opening our sense perceptions. For instance, loud city sounds—drilling through cement, the roar of trucks—can be potent and penetrating when we stay open to them. Heightening our sense perceptions allows us to connect with the power and potential in the world, which is the play of the five energies.

EXERCISE: WORKING WITH SENSE PERCEPTIONS

Sense perceptions include the sense organs or faculties (eyes, ears, nose, and so forth), the sense fields (experiences of seeing, hearing, smelling, and so forth), and sense objects (a tree, a song, the scent of a rose). You could enhance your sense faculties by working with the process of sense perception. By learning how to look, you discover how to see; by learning how to listen, you discover how to hear; by learning how to feel, you discover how to experience. Here is a three-stage process for experiencing sense perceptions more fully:

1. *Sense of being:* Establish a sense of being in the moment. Take in a deep breath and let it go. Let it cut through the cloud of distraction and preoccupation and put you on the spot.
2. *Sense of connecting:* Quickly engage one of your senses with an object. (Look at a tree, hear a car, touch your skin.) Be inquisitive; then you can see, hear, or touch.
3. *Sense of merging:* Establish communication between yourself and the object. Linger and merge, draw it into yourself, join your being with it. A dialogue or play begins, back and forth, without language.

Do these exercises with different sense perceptions in various environments. Use them as a quick break from work. Or take a walk. If you are with a friend, don't talk. Don't bring your dog; you'll have to invest too much energy in him. To heighten sense perceptions other than sight, let your friend lead you, blindfolded, on your walk. Keep your feet on the ground and feel the space around you. Stay tuned in to your senses. Touch into the play of energies. Opening to your sense perceptions in this way is refreshing and invigorating. Better than a cup of coffee!

15

Creativity: Expressing the Fullness of Being

As a dancer, teacher, therapist, and group facilitator, as well as with family and friends, I have found the creative process one of the most rewarding ways of discovering inner wealth. Creative expression sounds a deep chord that unearths aspects of ourselves that might otherwise go undiscovered. I have always enjoyed getting together with friends to play with expressive movement, music, song, text, whatever. Tired of dancing in studios and on stages, a dancer friend and I once put some money in a parking meter and danced in the parking space.

When we are being fully who we are—sensual, emotional, insightful—we respond with a creative gesture. Whether we are writing poetry, designing a house, planning an event, or choreographing a dance, the five energies provide a rich resource. Any artist is essentially connecting to the springboard of energy to create. But creativity also exists in ordinary moments throughout our lives. Being creative is simply letting our energy flow through us as best we can. As is said in Bali, "We have no art; we do everything as well as possible."

Because the creative process is intrinsically revealing and communicative, it is an effective way of experiencing the five energies more fully. Creativity both grounds and liberates what we feel. Whether we are preparing meals for our family or presenting a business report, our creativity is an expression of our perspective. The creative process is also intrinsically healing. One artist who had been depressed for several years after a traumatic experience said that working with the five energies brought color and energy back into her life. She was able to paint again.

I am always amused at flashes of inspiration that come to people when they're fashioning their environments. A few years ago I was sitting at the edge of a lake in a small resort town in Italian Switzerland. Across the street I noticed a row of ten cafés, all very much the same, except for one thing: the color of the tablecloths. I laughed when I noticed that the café with the red tablecloths was almost full, while the ones with green, blue, and white cloths were virtually empty! What did that café owner know about padma energy, I wondered?

THREE ASPECTS TO THE CREATIVE PROCESS

In teaching and working with creativity, I have found a five energies approach that encompasses three helpful steps: (1) opening to the moment and allowing inspiration, or vision, to arise (buddha/vajra); (2) elaborating on and embellishing the first idea (ratna); and (3) adding a personal touch (padma). Karma is present in finishing.

An open mind includes all possibilities without any one reference point. In an open space inspiration arises spontaneously, without strategy. What arises depends on who we are, where we are, what our energy is, and what we are trying to create. For example, in our inspiration to create a portrait of a friend—whether poetic or visual—we might clearly see her energy for the first time. Aha! The way ideas arise when we are in an open state of mind is like having a brainstorm. A word or an image comes to us "out of the blue."

Some of us are in the habit of jumping into our creative form prematurely, putting brush to canvas or pen to paper before having taken our seat. This is a dull and narrow way to create—not nearly as sparky and rich as tuning in to our creative possibilities in a spacious state of mind. On the other hand, some of us luxuriate in the spaciousness and then can't ground our ideas. We have ten ideas but initiate none. Being unable to connect our ideas to earth can seem confusing. Hanging out in space, we feel awkward, groundless, and uncomfortable. In some cases it helps to just do nothing for a while; in other cases it helps to bring ourselves down to earth by making a move—any move.

Next, we ground our inspiration by elaborating, developing, embellishing. As we work, our vision becomes full-blown. With the proper materials and skill, we put flesh on its bones. We bring its essence to flower. For example, we might fill out our friend's portrait by layering on her subtle coloring, calling forth her unique energy style.

The third aspect of the creative process is being in tune with our personal energy. Our unique manner of expression brings definition and shape to our creation. The portrait we create says as much about us as it does about the person depicted. Taking the same subject matter, different people will produce very different results. When several choreographers were asked to work with the theme of Adam and Eve, each of their dances was unique in its use of movement style, costume, and setting. Each showcased the individual choreographer's unique way of expressing himself.

I have come to trust these three aspects of working with creativity. They connect my sense of being with my creative process. Through using this approach, I've slowly learned to distinguish what arises from space and what arises from habitual patterns and discursive thought. I increasingly trust opening to space. Appropriate, direct, and unself-conscious action comes from that trust, whether I am creating a dance piece, preparing for a business meeting, planning a dinner, or writing an article. I've noticed that allowing the same sense of spaciousness to permeate my life ventilates every activity, bringing

vision and ease to everything I do. With this approach creativity becomes a natural part of life.

EXPLORING THE FIVE ENERGIES

Because direct experience speaks louder than words, working creatively evokes and heightens the five energies. The process of creation itself helps to transform the five energies. We are more likely to
touch their wisdom aspects through the creative process than
through any other means. To get a taste of creating with the five
energies, do the exercises at the end of the chapter. We will also look
at creating our world when working with others in chapter 16.

Bringing all energies into play is the most fruitional way of working. We can see this in the positive cyclical nature of the creative
process, which we discussed in chapter 11. The openness and all-
accommodating space of buddha become the inquisitive and understanding quality of vajra, which leads to the richness and possibility
of ratna, which become the appreciation of detail and refinement of
padma, which lead to the action of karma. In creative expression we
layer the families, beginning with one form of energy and adding di-
mension to our work with another and another.

One person in a workshop I taught created a wonderful example
of layering. As we worked with buddha-family energy, on a large
piece of paper she drew the faintest outline of a chair. As we worked
with the vajra family, the chair took on strong delineation and a real
sense of form. For ratna she added texture and color, creating a sense
of substantiality. For padma she added more color; now the chair was
inviting us to sit in it. I was amazed at what she came up with to
express karma energy: she cut out the chair and stood it up on the
floor.

MAITRI IN THE CREATIVE PROCESS

Maitri is an essential element in the creative process. When we feel
loving-kindness, we are able to express ourselves in a purer and more

brilliant way. Because we are accepting ourselves unconditionally, we tend to be less neurotic. When we feel good about ourselves, we can give full rein to our creative expression. To illustrate: for years I danced only in the friendly, familiar atmosphere of Naropa University. I usually felt good about my performances. When I was invited to perform in another setting, I sensed competitiveness and judgment in the air. Carrying this energy into my performance, I became judgmental of myself. Under these circumstances I did not enjoy performing nearly as much, nor did I perform as well.

A young, internationally known, Juilliard-trained violinist said she does not get nervous before performing. She doesn't worry about getting the notes right. What she mostly wants to do is communicate. Her sense of maitri toward herself allows her to ride the energy.

EXERCISE: CREATIVE EXPRESSION AND PLAY

You could work with creative expression either when you are focused on a particular family or with all the colors. Set aside some time. Pick an art form or choose a task that you want to accomplish in a more creative way. Get out the materials you will need.

You could play a musical instrument, dance, express yourself dramatically, write poetry, sing your own song, color (oil pastels or chalks, which produce bold, vibrant colors are good for this), make arrangements with objects, do an installation, or create a collage. You could also play selections of music or vocalize the sound for each family.

You might select certain aspects of the family to focus on: for example, the sense perception, the body part, the elemental sound, or the movement element. Focusing on a particular aspect of the family serves to orient the work.

You could also rearrange your house, plan your next business meeting, make a meal, or prepare for a party or wedding. If you are doing something like this, make sure you get to the point of actually carrying out the activity and don't just think about it.

Start by simply sitting still for about ten minutes. Enjoy the space. Touch in with your breath. Open to the moment and allow inspiration, or vision, to arise. Then play, elaborating on and embellishing the first idea. This is not about creating great art; it is about expressing who you are. Enjoy yourself. If you have friends working with the five energies, do it together. Have a color party!

PART FOUR

FIVE STYLES
OF RELATING
TO OTHERS

16

Embodying Energy and Creating Our World

There are limitless applications, both professional and personal, for five energies work. Although their goals may be different, people who work with others—therapists, teachers, businesspeople, facilitators, mediators, and health-care professionals—have found this work helpful. Couples, parents, and families have also found that a working knowledge of the five energies provides a potent dancing ground. With a mutual intention to use the five energies as ground for working together, the point is that the more aware we are of the five energies in ourselves, the more we open to the five energies in others. This potent combination of personal and interpersonal work is a lively journey.

In this section of the book, we will look at how to incorporate the five wisdom energies in relating with others. There are four essential aspects of this work: (1) manifesting the five energies in ourselves and the environment, (2) exchanging with another and recognizing his style, (3) knowing how to act, and (4) riding the energy. Each aspect provides the basic ground for a sane approach to working with the five energies. When we embody the energies in a sane way, we see people more clearly. Then we're more likely to know how to work with their mix of colors.

When we work with others, we become even more keenly attuned to how we embody the five energies. We find that they reflect back to us who we are all the time. When someone says, "What you said felt very sharp and abrupt" (vajra/karma) or "You seem to be whining and complaining all the time" (ratna) or "You're always so full of fun and play" (padma), we have a helpful framework in which to put his feedback to use. As we work with the five energies and begin to embrace who we are with unconditional friendliness, we begin to radiate the sanity of our mix of colors. No doubt we will not always manifest our brilliance, but at least we have some allegiance to doing so. This is what we can give to others. We can provide a container of radiant color. We can affect the environment, change the dynamics of energy, by how we manifest.

We can do this not only by embodying the energies and paying attention to our personal appearance—how we dress and groom ourselves—but by how we create our environment. The furnishings, textures, colors, lighting of any space have an impact on us. They have the power to change our state of mind. We can use this to our advantage. We can create environments of sanity, brilliant and colorful.

Spaciousness, clarity, richness, invitation, and workability are five different qualities that we can consciously bring into everything we do. Each of these qualities activates that particular energy in the environment around us. We can also create the ambience of each energy by physically changing the environment—moving furniture, decorating, adjusting the lighting.

Spaciousness

The first quality, related to the buddha family, is a sense of wholesomeness and basic goodness. It is a fundamental peace that says, "All is well." We can embody this quality in our personal presence by manifesting nonattachment and nonaggression, by being open to others. This atmosphere provides the space for people to express who they are without judgment or manipulation. Simply because we are providing room for them to be themselves, their situations could begin to feel workable to them. Creating a sense of open space and time invites a client, student, patient, or coworker into nowness. Entering the simplicity of the present moment is a tremendous relief. Spaciousness has the power to heal.

A spacious environment is an accepting environment. An important component is to actively surrender any sense of resistance you might feel toward the other person. Sometimes she will test how much you can handle. She needs to know how much of herself it is acceptable to show. If she senses that you are afraid, she will close down. In such a case, modeling bravery—an aspect of maitri—is the way to sustain the open environment. If you maintain the spacious environment by holding your seat without judging or attempting to control, it will bring you closer to the other person. Relief, gratitude, and a forward-moving relationship will follow.

Humor and playfulness are assets in creating a spacious environment. It helps to lighten up. Talk about the weather or something you know the other person enjoys. With my daughter, mentioning horses has the instantaneous effect of arousing her interest, engaging her out of her slump. Chatting—if not overdone—is a way of creating space, because it goes with the flow. Usually I am all too eager to get to the heart of the matter with a client. Small talk serves as a reminder to relax, let go, be who I am, without any roles. Sometimes I feel like a kayak following the river of someone's mind. I surrender to wherever it is we're going and at the same time attend keenly to every twist and turn that comes up.

In creating space, I also find it helpful to drop my sense of identity. Reminding myself to "Let go of being the facilitator" or "Stop mothering" or "Don't be directive" allows me to momentarily relinquish my image of myself as well as my agenda. I no longer feel obligated to be "on." At the same time, letting go of these reference points puts me very much on the spot, as if I were flying by the seat of my pants. This willingness to hang out beyond what is comfortable, in the realm of not knowing, is openness.

To create a spacious atmosphere in a room, simplicity is the key. Clear out any unnecessary objects with the idea of there being "enough." (Too little feels sparse and barren.) You can also create a sense of spaciousness in your appearance. When I know I am going to be working with people for a longer time—as when I'm teaching the same group for a week—I begin by dressing in a very simple way. Rather than imposing myself on the group, I create space for them.

Clarity and Inquisitiveness

The next qualities that we can consciously bring into our environment, clarity and inquisitiveness, are related to the vajra family. The best way to awaken someone's intelligence is to awaken our own. When we are feeling sharp and clear, we radiate those qualities to others. Sometimes we can express our clarity by saying how we see things. Even more helpful may be to create an atmosphere of inquisitiveness. Ask questions. The right question at the right moment can pierce to the heart of the matter in a flash. Asking a clear question allows someone to access his own clarity. It empowers him and captures his curiosity. Questioning is a good way to model an inquisitive and discriminating mind for others.

In the outer mandala clarity and inquisitiveness are what we draw on in placing objects and furniture in a room, creating both spaciousness and order. For instance, clustering plants, paintings, or seashells together leaves more open space in the rest of the room. These vajra qualities come in handy in attending to the shape and texture of eye-catching objects like a sculpture, flowers, rocks, or crystals—all of which have the potential to capture our mind, provoke our intelligence, and wake us up. However, too much clarity—as in too many bold colors, sharp lines, and metallic textures—can make a room feel cold. On days when I want to manifest clarity, I might wear blue clothes with simple lines, accentuated by silver jewelry.

Resourcefulness and Richness

The qualities of the ratna family that we use to work with our inner and outer mandalas are resourcefulness and richness. There is no one way to relate to another person; it is an ongoing dance from moment to moment. Being resourceful, we can continually tap our inner resources—life experience, intelligence, and skills—as well as a positive sense that the world is full of possibility. Resourcefulness and richness also mean being able to draw from our area of expertise or a body of knowledge in giving someone what he might need most in the moment, such as an answer to a computer problem. We enrich others by offering the best of who we are. Stories, images, and metaphors are also good ways of communicating a sense of richness.

For instance, living for eight months in Nepal, where there was no family entertainment, my husband, John, and I started telling stories to our three-year-old Chandra. We enjoyed this so much that storytelling continued when we were back home. Quite spontaneously, I created a central character called KC, who soon became identified as (Karuna) Chandra. At some point we told Chandra that it was her turn, and she started telling stories as well.

By happenstance, I discovered that this was a way to communicate with her, which had an amusing result. Since John and I had become upset by her seemingly endless accumulation of stuffed animals, I wove that into a story. The gist of it was that KC collected so many stuffies on her bed that she had to sleep on the floor, then move out of her room into the hall, then outside into the shed. When she discovered that she could be generous and give some of her stuffies to her friends, she was able to move back into her room. Chandra absorbed this story quietly. However, the next day, when it was her turn to tell a story, all those stuffies came back! I was beside myself with laughter at the incorrigibility of her ratna energy.

Like any family, we sometimes feel bored with our usual ways of interacting. At these times we might decide to color together. It's not that we're artists; we just want another way of being together besides talking or watching a movie. So we take out the colored pencils and chalks and sit at the table and color. Then we show one another what we have done. We laugh and make jokes and appreciate one another's colors in this way. Our family is enriched when we are resourceful in being together, whether telling stories or coloring.

We can create a sense of richness in our home and work spaces by using colorful fabrics, plants, and warm, indirect lighting. If this approach is overdone, it feels indulgent; you'll know when it's just enough because you'll feel a sense of richness that isn't overwhelming. When I want to manifest richness on my person, I wear bright, warm colors, often with floral designs, and gold jewelry.

Genuine Friendship and Invitation

The fourth aspect of creating a wakeful environment is cultivating genuine friendship, which brings in the energy of the padma family. Extending ourselves through openheartedness invites others to a more intimate relationship. This invitation can be an oasis in a desert for them. It creates an environment in which—as our clients, students, or professional associates—they are invited to share their world without holding back.

Padma energy magnetizes and melts people. When my heart breaks open toward someone—feeling his pain or his joy—that person opens to me as well. Our energies merge. It's like falling in love, for however brief a time. This is the essence of genuine relationship—simply being human together. Genuine friendship is compassionate. It feels like coming home to the heart. It has nothing to do with the particular roles we might have in relation to each other.

In therapy I find that when I make friends with a client, our relationship becomes a healing tool. Dropping my role of organizational consultant as much as possible allows more connection—the direct, unobstructed sharing of energy. Radiating friendliness and sharing myself in a simple way softens any encounter. I've experienced the same warmth, sharing, playfulness, and intimacy with students and clients that I feel with my closest friends.

I'll never forget one day when, particularly touched by a client's story, I began to cry. Although she herself was not ready to feel the sadness of her situation, she playfully picked up the ever-present box of tissues and handed it to me. I was not embarrassed. She was having a hard time being touched by feeling; I was modeling it.

Using the energy of padma, we can create spaces that are enormously inviting, with soft contours, warm colors, and subtle lighting. If not overdone (when the effect can seem indulgent), warmth and softness in an environment invite us to be together in more intimate ways. To arouse padma energy in my appearance, I like to wear clothes that make me feel attractive. Warm colors, particularly red, and attention-getting jewelry—my velvet heart pin or my colorful hummingbird pin or dangling earrings—are what I choose.

Workability

The fifth way we can awaken the environment is through workability, a karma-family quality. It sometimes seems to me that 99 percent of our conversations revolve around complaining about how badly things are going or trying to figure out how to fix them. The workable approach is that there is no problem so solid that it can't be penetrated. When we are not daunted by someone's predicament or an organization's difficulties, we reflect this sense of workability.

We can model workability by offering people creative options about how situations might be approached. When people are experiencing a problem, we can remind them of solutions that have worked for them in the past. For example, Annelie often forgets that what has always helped her out of her depression is doing sitting meditation. Michael stays bottled up and forgets that talking to someone often makes him feel better. Elizabeth knows that she starts to binge on alcohol when she stops going to her AA meetings. By offering a gentle reminder of the workability of a problem, we are creating an atmosphere of friendliness and action.

A karma environment is an efficient one. For example, we set up

our workplace to be useful to ourselves and others—desk, file drawers, phone. We have on hand whatever we need to accomplish the
task of the day. The space is organized so it functions well for what
we have to do, which doesn't necessarily mean that it's bereft of the
other colors. To express workability in my appearance, I wear clothes
suited to the requirements of whatever work I'm doing.

These five ways of creating an environment are always at play in
our relationships with others. Cultivating awareness of them allows
us to bring into play the mandala of energies on both the inner and
outer levels. It gives us the opportunity to strike out in different directions when we feel "stuck" in an interpersonal situation. By experimenting with these five qualities at different times, in different
situations, and with different balances, we are likely to discover new
ways of making meaningful and mutually beneficial relationships.

EXERCISE: EMBODYING THE ENERGIES
AND CREATING YOUR WORLD

This exercise is one that you could work with over time. First of all,
reflect on the place where you work or live with others. See which
energies are present and which need cultivation. Try layering the
energies: start with a sense of clear-span space, then very precisely
introduce only the basic structural elements you need: desk, chair,
sofa, whatever. Then add whatever enriches: plants, rugs, curtains,
lighting. Then add whatever is particularly magnetizing; art objects,
colorful pillows, a flower arrangement, a conversation piece. Then
make sure the space functions for the job you intend.

You can also be more conscious about wearing clothes suited to
the occasion. Pay attention to the energy you are trying to create.

Most important, now that you are familiar with the energies, be
more aware of the shifts in energy needed to relate to a particular
situation. Does the situation call for spaciousness, clarity, enrichment, warmth, or a sense of workability? More than likely, it requires
some combination of these.

17

Seeing It Their Way, Seeing Them

Our own defenses are most often what keep us prisoner to the illusion that we are separate from others. We can experience this sense of barrier in numerous ways: we don't care (buddha), we are too busy (karma), it's not within our job description (vajra), we don't like the other person (padma), or we feel overwhelmed (ratna). It is interesting to be curious about how we project our version of the world onto others, because our projection also makes it impossible to see another person for who she is. I find that I can make genuine contact with someone else only when I am willing to drop my own story line and agenda. Although doing this takes conscious effort, it enables me to put myself in her shoes, empathize, and resonate with her energy, which opens me to our interconnectedness.

EXCHANGE

The natural process of opening to our interconnectedness in this way is called exchange—the direct, unobstructed sharing of energy with another. Opening to and exchanging with another is similar to opening to our sense perceptions, which connects us to the world of phenomena. The unobstructed quality of this process comes only from tuning in to the energy of the present moment, which is always available beyond our own ego wall of thoughts, concepts, ideas, and projections.

It is helpful to know that exchange is always happening, regardless of whether we are conscious of doing it. When we are not aware of the exchange, it is confusing. We mix with someone's energy, and it's not clear whether we're in his movie or our own. For this reason partners may sometimes feel the need to spend some time away from their loved one in order to rediscover themselves.

When we are aware of exchange—equally aware of our energy as well as the other person's—it becomes a useful tool. Exchange is a present-moment interface with another person. It is opening to the moment with the intention of relating. Tension arose between a used-car salesman and my husband and me when we told him we weren't buying his car because we'd found a better deal. Needless to say, he wasn't happy. When I asked him what he would do if he were in our situation, an exchange occurred and the energy softened. He smiled and admitted he would do exactly what we were doing.

Being aware of the five energies is useful in practicing exchange, because it helps us move toward perception and away from projection. When we can see the play of colors for what it is, our opening to another can be straightforward rather than confusing. For example, if our friend is in a hell realm because her love affair is over, we can maintain our connection with her and yet still be who we are. Exchange can happen only when we can join without becoming enmeshed. We can feel the raw energy (in this example our friend's pain) without buying the projection (her story line or her sense of blame). This allows us to stay with the wholeness of other person's energy without fueling its confused quality.

Compassion is an important component of exchange. Compassion is what opens us to another person's suffering, confusion, and pain. Underlying compassion is the warmth of maitri—unconditional loving-kindness. When we experience maitri for someone else, compassion naturally arises. Rather than defending ourselves against his pain, we can enter into it.

In any relationship there are three patterns of energy: our colors, the other person's colors, and the colors we create together. The colors we create together are the exchange. For example, Paula's basic energy is buddha with some ratna possibilities. She brings these into relationship with each of her family members. With her karma husband, she gives him a lot of space to be as active as he wants to be. They also share a love for remodeling and decorating their house. His activity rouses her out of her more complacent way of being, and she proves to be quite resourceful in gathering materials and brings a sense of richness to the work. This is how the exchange manifests between her buddha/ratna and his karma. With her vajra son, she listens for many hours (buddha) while he talks about his dissertation in environmental ecology. He has a lot of high ideals and often becomes overly opinionated and negative (vajra). She shows acceptance and appreciation in her interactions with him. This pacifies him and gives him a sense of positive outlook and possibility. She, in turn, gets quite stimulated by all his ideas. Paula and her teenage padma daughter can be very intimate and have heart-to-heart talks. Paula is a good listener; it is just what her quite emotional daughter needs. She is also very available to help with her daughter's many creative projects (buddha space and ratna resourcefulness with padma).

Since energy exchange dissolves barriers, the energies of Paula and her family members blend together. Paula and her husband have a buddha/ratna/karma blend; with her son there is a buddha/ratna/vajra blend; with her daughter there is a buddha/ratna/padma blend. They can relate to one another's energy because, for the most part, they are open and in exchange with one another. There is a merging of colors. If the members of this family were not in exchange, their energies would get more solidified and polarized.

We can also dissolve barriers in our work world, however much it may be driven by intense competitiveness. A president of a successful young company who has worked with this material says that transcending the idea of competition is a successful business strategy. When you exchange with a potential competitor and see the sanity in what she is doing, you could appreciate her and be supportive. You could also see that what you have to offer is different, complementary. When you connect with inherent richness in yourself and the world, you see that there is room for everyone. This is a ratna take on a situation; ratnas love to share and appreciate.

RECOGNIZING STYLE

Recognizing someone else's style is a way to enter into his world and see more clearly both his sanity and his confusion. It gives us a map of his inner landscape—the valleys of his distress and the peaks of his brilliance. We might begin to see, for example, how thoroughly his sanity is buried in emotional upheaval or tied up in intellectual knots.

Recognition arises not from intellectual analysis but from intuitive perception. It is "grokking" someone—understanding her energy beyond concept. For instance, if we focus only on what the other person is saying, we don't feel her energy. To feel her energy fully, we need to open to everything about her—including her tone of voice, the style of her presentation, her personal appearance, and her body language. When we have this kind of complete insight, we will experience a tangible physical sensation of connection with her. There's a visceral sense of "clicking in" with our intellect and our intuition. When I feel completely touched by someone, I often get tears in my eyes. Something has just come into focus in a heartfelt and mind-penetrating way. These moments of connection are powerful: they resonate over time.

Our experience of one another can often be confusing, both because all of us have many color possibilities to begin with and because a change in setting may evoke different energies than we are used to seeing. For example, if ordinarily we relate to Bill in a context that engages his dominant energy—work—we may be mystified when at a party we meet his neurotic mask. As we practice working with the energy dynamics of the five families, however, we can be more open to the full mix of colors that someone is presenting. To this end, curiosity is helpful. We can ask ourselves questions like, "Which energy seems to be more basic, which more situational? What is the dominant emotional tone? What layering and merging are going on? When is the person more at ease or more in struggle? What is the quality of his sanity? What is he passionate about?"

When I am trying to pick up on someone's colors, I also use feeling as my guide. How does the other person make me feel? Do I feel as if I have no space? (Neurotic ratna.) Do I feel that no matter what I do, it is hard to make contact? (Neurotic vajra or buddha.) Do I delight in this person's company? (Sane padma.) Do I feel completely confused by what she is saying? (Neurotic padma.) Do things come into focus, become clearer when I am with this person? (Sane vajra.) Is what I sense her energy or my reaction to her energy? For example, if the person sitting in front of me is intensely angry, I might feel not anger but fear or, perhaps later, sadness. Being inquisitive—about both myself and the other person—helps. A grounding question is "What is this?"

The process I'm describing is not intended to pigeonhole someone's energy style. I learn more if I play with it. Usually I "try on" different colors to see what fits. Sometimes I eliminate certain colors that obviously don't correspond to the energy I am picking up. There is nothing "wrong" about my choices; I am experimenting, playing. Once I recognize someone's coloring, I have a sense of the world he inhabits, both neurotic and sane. Clicking into someone's style gives me the space to be more present. I can relax into the particular color he is expressing. I don't have to distract myself by trying to figure out what makes him tick at the moment.

For instance, when I first knew her, I thought a friend of mine was very padma because she always talked about her relationships with men. It was only later in our relationship that I saw how ratna she was. Her neediness and her feeling of insubstantiality created a continual drive to fill the space—with people (especially boyfriends), knowledge, and possessions. At one point she had five boyfriends! When she found some stability in her relationships, another aspect of her came to the fore—a keen intellect that loved to do academic research (vajra). Over time I have seen that ratna and vajra are basic to her but that padma is also in the mix, sometimes as a delightful enhancement to attract her many boyfriends and sometimes as a mask to hide her pain.

EXERCISE: EXCHANGE

Practice the exercise at the end of chapter 13, working with maitri and transmutation. Very specifically do it for someone you know or a difficult relationship in which you are involved, one that evokes strong emotion. Over time you will discover that your relationship with this person will change. Finding more openness in yourself allows more openness in relation to him or her.

EXERCISE: RECOGNIZING STYLE

In a light-handed way, try recognizing the personality styles of people you know. Try out one energy for a while. Say to yourself, Jack is vajra. As you exchange with him, see whether it fits. Maybe he is only vajra at work. Maybe in going to dinner at his house, you find he has a lot of ratna. Over time see whether you can perceive Jack more clearly and enter his world more fully by recognizing his mix of colors.

18

Knowing How to Act

Through having learned to accept ourselves in all our shades of sanity and neurosis, we have begun to trust our innate intelligence. By having cultivated "staying power" with our own emotions, we are now able to listen to ourselves and stay in open dialogue with someone else at the same time. Most important, we can do this without getting distracted by the other person's energy. We can hold our seat. And we can remember that not knowing what to do is fertile ground for knowing what to do.

If someone is commandeering the space with her stories and personal problems, we may feel overwhelmed, but we don't react. If someone flies at us with anger, we can feel the anger without lashing back. Through the power of our own ability to stay with an emotion without acting it out or suppressing it, we can ride the particular roller coaster of someone else's energy. This gives us the freedom to use our finely tuned psychophysical barometer in the service of others. This tool is useful in telling when others are open or closed. We can see their sanity and their confusion; we can also see how they teeter on the edge between them. Sometimes we might choose to align with their sanity by drawing it out. Other times we can mirror their neurosis, reflecting back to them where they are stuck.

ALIGNING WITH SANITY BY DRAWING IT OUT

Aligning with sanity is having allegiance to the wisdom aspect of energy. It creates the potential for the wisdom aspect of the energies to emerge in others. If our own allegiance to sanity is unwavering, we can bring the other person along. If we stay with the attitude that someone is fundamentally OK, he will start to believe it, too. Recognizing someone's basic nature is helpful, in that it enables us to relate more skillfully to drawing it out. Appreciating the intelligence of the person's dominant quality allows his other qualities to become more integrated. We can radiate our sanity and become a container of maitri, with all our colors, for others.

Even in the briefest encounter, allegiance to basic sanity can have an impact. For example, you see an acquaintance on the street and ask her how she is. She says she's fine, but in chatting with her, you become aware that she is mumbling and fidgeting and can't look you in the eye. Sensing a cover-up, you drop any self-preoccupation, become present for her, and continue your exchange. Then the conversation takes on more depth. You find out how she really is. She is grieving her mother, who recently died. Gradually, in dialogue, the clouds are acknowledged: her anger that there is no one there for her, how alone and abandoned she feels. You ride her energy, experiencing the heat of her anger as well as her genuine sadness. You stay aligned with her intelligence at feeling sad about her mother's passing. At some point in your conversation, your friend feels seen and heard. Through the exchange she no longer feels alone, and she has also honored her feeling of sadness.

It is possible to do an on-the-spot energy exchange that takes in the neurosis of someone else's style and sends out the wisdom aspect—nourishing the inherent intelligence of who he or she is. If someone is angry (vajra neurosis), I point out the intelligence at play, highlighting the good reasons the person has to be angry. If someone was neglected and abused as a child, for example, it is completely natural—healthy, in fact—for the clear, sharp energy of anger to emerge. When someone has just been fired, anger is inevitable, a response to the "death" of a situation. When we acknowledge the intelligence of anger, we are recognizing the wisdom aspect of the energy, which opens the door to transformation. When we align with the sanity, the neurosis will drop away. Often we don't even have to deal with it.

Here is another example of aligning with sanity by drawing it out. Roger came to therapy with me on the recommendation of a teacher at his vocational school. He had little interest in classes and was often tardy, sleepy, or absent. In our first session we talked about how he didn't want to be at school because it was boring and sometimes overwhelming. He had a long history of needing stimulation to keep awake, although he had recently given up coffee. We talked about sleep habits and diet.

At the end of the session, I asked Roger what he wanted to get out of our meetings. He said he wanted to learn to be on time, though he hated the idea. I told him it didn't interest me to work with him on an issue that didn't interest him. He said he'd also like to be able to follow through on projects. We decided that, in the week between sessions, he would be inquisitive about his diet. In this session I was very bored, picking up on his boredom, lethargy, and general lack of interest. I pegged him as having buddha energy.

Roger came to the second session wanting to discuss many ideas about diet, which took up almost half the session. Even though I was bored and kept wondering whether this was really what he wanted to talk about, I let him ramble on. What I saw was that all his thoughts about diet were philosophical: he wanted to eat lower on the food chain, he didn't want to support cruelty to animals, he wanted to eat ecologically. He didn't relate his diet to his own health and vitality. This is how I discovered his passion, his intelligence.

Our conversation about diet was my first glimpse of Roger's dominant vajra quality, which was to become more vivid as the session went on. For example, it turned out that the novel he had mentioned writing in the first session was essentially a philosophical treatise about the evolution of consciousness. Several times he talked about his many different interests and his love of research. He confided his vision of becoming a "planetary therapist." Although he had many ideas, however, he realized that he rarely followed through with any of them.

On the one hand, because Roger needed to feel he was the best, he would abandon a project if he felt someone else could do it just as well. In this way he was turning his critical vajra eye upon himself in the form of judgments. On the other hand, he felt there was very little that was important enough for him to do. In this way he was stuck in vajra arrogance tinged with boredom. I suggested that, with his high ideals and big vision, no wonder he was dissatisfied with everything. It made sense that he would be bored and sleepy in class.

When he heard this, Roger gasped and tears filled his eyes. "That's it, that's it," he said, as he touched his chest. "You have really hit the center." The only way we were able to arrive at this place was that, throughout the session, I kept discounting his negativity about himself and supporting what was strong in him, his passion. I began to see his brilliance—in this case his vajra intellect. In the end so did he. The intensity of the vajra energy was blocking his fullness because he was turning it against himself. He needed to make friends with it.

In a therapy session with Patricia, she summed up her dilemma in the statement, "I don't want to be alone, and yet I can't imagine anyone wanting to be with me. I'm too sick. I feel overwhelmed and wrong—as if what I am is bad." Though she appeared to be bright and capable, I was struck by the intense attitude of internal poverty Patricia was expressing. It felt like ratna neurosis to me.

So I started to look for her resourcefulness. We devoted whole sessions to exploring what was rich and plentiful in her life, and I gave her homework to do as well. She needed to discover her inner wealth for herself—her ability to make her apartment look beautiful, her flair for dressing, her talent for cooking. Finally she was no longer able to deny her treasury of resources. Her sanity overtook her neurosis. When we parted company, she had a new job and bright possibilities.

I work with a very professional and dynamic group of people at the National Institute for School Improvement in the Netherlands. They work as trainers, coaches, and facilitators with teachers and school administrators. Here is how one of them has connected to his own sanity and fullness of being, seen it in others, and has aligned with sanity: "This work enables me to see new aspects of other people as well as working with loving-kindness, compassion, and nowness. I sense more and more that what I do is an expression of who I am. I cannot rely anymore on tricks and techniques. I am only able to do what I believe in." Another observed, "I am realizing the importance of nowness and connecting in the moment. My workshops have gained more freshness because I start from what is and not from what I want it to be. I see the individuals in my groups more [clearly,] so, in this way, my workshops have gained depth."

Likewise, aligning with sanity supports an organization. After I did the exercises at the end of chapter 11 with a company of database designers, the group continued to explore their personal aspirations as well as those of the organization. There was bonding, shared vision, and a strong sense of being recognized as full human beings. Their best was being seen. As Andrew, an administrator, said, "My intelligence has never been so acknowledged and utilized in a work situation." That organization will have no problem with retention!

In therapy deep work is encouraged; in schools and organizations the focus is on bringing out full human potential; in everyday life we can align with sanity by drawing it out in simple ways. When we encounter someone who seems frazzled—a grocery store checkout person, a waitress, a bank teller—we can smile, ask her how she is doing, and wish her a good day. Sounds corny but it works.

ALIGNING WITH SANITY BY
MIRRORING NEUROSIS

The other way to align with sanity is to work with someone's neurosis. Mirroring neurosis means seeing someone's neurosis clearly and then penetrating its stuckness. In doing so, we welcome the other person's neurotic aspects without trying to fix them. As it can make someone feel quite vulnerable, first we have to establish a ground of trust. In mirroring, we can ask someone to describe clearly what happens when he begins to close down. What triggers it? What happens next? When does it become a full-blown drama? What was his part in creating the situation? What did it feel like? Then we reflect back to him what he just said. Because we are in exchange, we can simply offer him a clear mirror, free of opinions and judgments. If we have picked up on the color of his neurosis, we might exaggerate it a bit so he can see his energy more clearly. With this approach we can bring the struggle into awareness in a gentle way.

We can balance these two ways of aligning with sanity. In using the technique of drawing out the sanity, sometimes we can redefine each moment toward sanity, no matter how bleak the situation. This is a good way to establish the ground of brilliant sanity. At other times we can delve into someone's pain and simply be there with her, which may allow the space for her sanity to emerge.

Mirroring neurosis can be trickier, because when we use this technique, the other person might feel criticized or attacked. The effect of our action is that he is now on the defensive. When we use mirroring skillfully, however, the other person will be able to see for himself where he is stuck.

Whether we are aligning with sanity by drawing it out or by mirroring neurosis, bringing warmth and relaxation into our work with others is the basic ground. In doing this, maitri and compassion are the most basic skillful means.

WORKING WITH SANITY AND NEUROSIS
IN FIVE COLORS

Here are a few guidelines for working with each family's neurosis as well as aligning with its sanity, in ourselves and in others.

Vajra

Since the passion of vajra energy is to know, the symptom of vajra stuckness is a network of intellectual knots. To pop this neurosis, we need to simplify the convoluted logic. We can make a straightforward statement as to what we see as the essence of the logic. We can bring the energy down to earth by connecting the ideas to the immediate situation—like talking to Roger about his diet. It also helps to create a sense of context and perspective—like suggesting to Roger that it was his high ideals and big vision that made him dissatisfied and bored in class. Roger needed a logical explanation. For some people cutting the knots of vajra might involve bypassing the mind altogether. We could suggest physical exercise, for example—anything to get vajras out of their heads. Introducing another energy is often helpful: we could provide the sense of richness and possibility of ratna or the charm and playfulness of padma.

Aligning with the sanity of vajra people involves appreciating their clarity. Giving them a different perspective or an overview—Roger's big vision in light of his classroom boredom—dissolves their sense of conflict with a situation, allowing them to feel at peace. When they see the large view in a simple way, they can relax.

Ratna

Constricted ratnas display a poverty mentality characterized by a sense of inadequacy. Since ratna people are comfort-oriented, we want to put them at their ease. We can become an accommodating presence. Because they have issues of self-worth, we need to reassure them and at the same time cut through their self-pity. We can build them up and nurture them. However, we have to be careful that they don't feed on our attention as a way to indulge their neediness.

One way of aligning with the sanity of ratna people would be to help them discover their inner richness and resources—as with Patricia above.

Padma

Neurotic padma energy tends to be fluctuating, scattered, and unstable; it needs to be focused. Padma emotions need to be allowed expression as well as pacified. They need to be clarified but not indulged. Padmas require structure and continuity, because it is hard for them to make decisions. They have to engage their passion without losing sight of the danger of getting caught up in or intoxicated by it. For padmas every situation must have some charm. If life feels too routine, they miss the sense of freshness. We don't want to eliminate their passion; we want to cultivate it, refine it.

Since padma people take pleasure in the intensity of their pain, one way of aligning with their sanity is to suggest that they go deeper into it—by writing poetry or listening to music, for instance. Since they are very sensitive to connections and always want to know whether we like them, we need to reassure them that we care.

Karma

When karma people are stuck, they become paranoid and suspicious. To help them wake up to their wisdom, we need to work with their distrust of others. We can gain their trust by being consistent and straightforward. This can be frustrating, because just when we feel they are going along with us, they might become paranoid again. Also, we might find that there is little to talk about; karmas are doers.

We can align with karma sanity by giving karma people lots of things to do, as long as there is the coherence of good intentions. We could suggest activities that slow them down and provide more space in their lives, like massage or meditation.

Buddha

People with frozen buddha energy are confused and vague, so it is frustrating to work with them. They shroud their sanity in ignorance, passivity, and an unwillingness to relate to what is happening. They are sleepy and immovable, like Roger in the example above. Because they are the most unresponsive to stimulation, it is hard to make contact with them, draw them out, or get them to participate. People caught in this way need a push, something that will shake them up, a sharp disruption of their habitual pattern. Stimulation is the ticket here. Discovering what kind of stimulation would work is a matter of finding their "hook," what will draw them out—intellect, seduction, inspiration, or whatever. The process of awakening them has to be active and gradual. It takes patience and much prodding.

Aligning with the sanity of buddha people might involve sitting quietly or meditating with them. We need to talk to them in simple language. After discovering their "hook," we can be more active.

EXERCISE: WORKING WITH SANITY AND NEUROSIS IN FIVE COLORS

Decide when you want to do this exercise. It could be for a week, a day, or even an hour. Try it with whomever you encounter during the week or pick one person with whom you want to try it out: a therapeutic client, a coworker, or your spouse or child.

Whatever this person brings to you, become a container of unconditional acceptance and friendliness. Be open to who he is, what he says, and what he does. If you have worked with the exercise in the last chapter on recognizing style, see whether you can identify what energy he is manifesting. It is also fine if you can't. However closed or stuck his energy, see the inherent intelligence in it. Acknowledge that you recognize his sanity. If the time feels right, you could also reflect back to the person in a simple way what you see him saying and doing that creates his confusion. Then let it go.

19

Riding the Energy

OPENING TO THE MANDALA

In the energetic matrix of mandala, there is the possibility of both confusion/chaos and sanity/order. When we learn to relax and open into the whole spectrum, in the moment, we experience neurosis and sanity as coexistent. As we attend to our experience with awareness and maitri, wisdom arises from the confusion. This is how we transmute energy. Although this process of transmutation may take years of practice, it can also happen in a flash. However long it takes, once we begin to experience our basic nature of brilliant sanity, we start aligning with it. Then we can learn to touch in with it on the spot. We can learn to align ourselves with the totality of the five energies as a way out of our constricted ego sphere. We can learn to help others do the same. We can begin to see that all of us are connected in a larger context, as part of a vaster totality.

Living in the mandala means giving up the reference point of "me." It is living in the moment, being able to manifest without reference back to a self. This means learning to drop the context and object of whatever emotion we're experiencing. Then we just hang out in space with its energy. This is how we glimpse the totality of the mandala. We relax and allow the energy to be as it is, without trying to control or influence it. Letting ourselves be and allowing ourselves to fit into the big picture—without manipulating or scheming—is a powerful experience. This is how we learn to ride the energies of the mandala.

AUSPICIOUS COINCIDENCE

The experience of power and magic that comes from riding the confluence of energies of the moment is called "auspicious coincidence." Here is an example. At times I have wondered, "How is it that I am here writing this book? What was the confluence of circumstances that brought me here? What were the choices to go in this direction rather than another?" When we open to the matrix of energies, we can ride the coincidence of the moment. The favorable circumstances that prevailed in my life that led to writing this book include reading the passage about the energies in *Cutting through Spiritual Materialism*, being invited to teach at Naropa, sitting in Martha's living room when she popped the idea of writing a book into my head, finding out that my editor-to-be lived only blocks away from me, and having the time and space in my life to do it.

Conventional thinking has it that being active means exerting energy to manipulate the world the way we want it to go. As a result, we often become confused trying to decide how to act. But in fact, we don't have to exert energy; we only need to join with it. When we know how to ride the energies of the moment, our actions are a spontaneous and appropriate response to whatever situation we're in. In each of the moments mentioned above, I had a choice: either to deny the opportunity that was presenting itself or to ride the wave of coincidence. The world presents us with occasions to which we can respond directly, in tune with what is going on. It's like kayaking or skiing. When we surrender to the natural flow of energy, we don't have to think about what to do next.

RIDING THE MOMENT: FOUR POWERS

Magic happens when our inner and outer mandalas are in total alignment. When working with the energies, we see that that magic has four powers, which are the sane action, the wisdom activity, of each energy family. The powers for each family are as follows:

1. Buddha and vajra combine in the calmness and evenness of just being, with a pacifying, unyielding, immovable quality.
2. Ratna is enriching and resourceful.
3. Padma is magnetizing, embracing, and inspiring.
4. Karma is actualizing or fulfilling, destroying anything that is too fixated.

Acting in accord with these four powers is fundamentally beneficial beyond personal territory. When we are hooked into the energy of the moment, there is no "me" anymore. We lose ourselves. This is the magic dance of no self. People call it a "high" or "being in the groove."

With egoless action we respond to whatever is needed, without hesitation. If somebody is coming at us with aggression, we pacify. If we need to catch a plane, we move fast. If somebody needs to be drawn out, we magnetize. If something needs to be stopped in its tracks, we destroy. On a crowded subway padma schmooze is not appropriate; karma street smarts take command. We don't impose ourselves on a situation and try to change it; we merge with the situation and act. In a given situation all four powers can come into play, as in the following example.

When a dispute over salaries arose between the faculty and administration of the small college where Gerald is dean of faculty, he chose nonaction. He observed what was going on, listened to everyone, and did not take sides. Because they had the space to be heard, the faculty and administration calmed down (pacifying). There was a peaceful ground from which to proceed. Gerald also gained some clarity himself during the course of hearing everyone's view.

At some point Gerald called a meeting between the faculty and administration. He asked that they all look at the big picture, not just salaries, and invited proposals aimed at creating more wealth for the school (enriching). In doing this, he recognized the poverty mentality inherent in the situation and skillfully directed the group toward its richness and resourcefulness.

Next, Gerald invited a few people to work closely with him (magnetizing). His own excitement about moving things forward stimulated their interest. It inspired them to look at the possible resources available for improving their situation. Gerald did not entertain anyone's poverty mentality (destroying) but continually steered everyone involved toward active engagement in making things happen for the benefit of all.

It is important to remember that working with the five energies and four powers is not a system to use by rote. It is just another way to be in our daily lives. The big secret is that magic and power are extraordinarily ordinary when you are being fully who you are. The more we make a project out of the five energies, the less genuine our connection to them will be. Working with the five energies is an expansion of our awareness and a spontaneous way of perceiving the world. It is a path of insight, not a conceptual overlay. We could think of working with the five energies as a way to contemplate whatever we encounter, an opportunity to see the world through rainbow glasses.

This book is an invitation to dance your own dance, sing your own song, all within the vivid display of the mandala, the energetic sphere. It is an invitation to create your world and work compassionately with others. Most of all, it is an invitation to ride the energy of the moment and to celebrate the brilliance of the five wisdom energies. I hope you will be inspired to discover for yourself the richness of living in a multicolored world. Please enjoy yourself!

EXERCISE: RIDING THE ENERGY OF THE MOMENT

Every so often during your day, just stop what you are doing and open to the moment. Start by taking a deep breath. Ride the energy. Appreciate the auspicious coincidence of who you are and what you are doing at that very moment.

The Five Wisdom Energies at a Glance

Have fun with these. Although many of these qualities are traditional, others represent possibilities or suggestions.

VAJRA QUALITIES

Physical Manifestations

- **People:** leaders, diplomats, scientists, surgeons, dentists, watchmakers, engineers, computer programmers, samurai
- **Style of dress:** simple lines, solid colors or geometric patterns, ornamentation with clean-cut lines
- **Sense perception:** sight
- **Areas of the body:** forehead, chest
- **Health problems:** headache, stiff and rigid body, lack of appetite, malnourishment
- **Element:** water
- **Season:** winter
- **Time of day:** dawn
- **Color:** blue
- **Shape:** circle
- **Movement elements:** spatial and bodily design, time (rhythm)
- **Landscapes/environments:** high mountains and cities, interiors that are well ordered
- **Animals:** eagles, sharks, swordfish

Expression

- **Passion**: wanting to know
- **Sane activity:** pacifying
- **Neurotic activities:** intellectualizing, overanalyzing
- **Mode:** mental
- **Style:** conceptual
- **Intensified emotion:** anger, hot or cold
- **Breakdown point:** logic becoming convoluted
- **Sense of insufficiency:** not feeling right or perfect
- **Defense mechanisms:** sticking to own concepts, rigid and doctrinaire, distancing self from others
- **Realm:** hell, hot or cold
- **Intensified preoccupation:** trying to make things as they should be
- **Fear:** emotional intimacy
- **Sources of security:** knowing the answers, being right
- **Relationships:** impersonal, compassionate, aggressive
- **Cultures:** decorum, order, Japanese, Scandinavian, German, English
- **Art styles:** classical, neoclassical, formalist, conceptual, abstract
- **Visual art:** precision and geometry; bold, bright colors; graphic art; photography; filmmaking
- **Architecture:** clean lines, sharply delineated spaces, refinement, uplifting and light, mirrors and crystals, bright colors, stained-glass windows
- **Dance:** concern with shape, space, and time; ballet
- **Literature:** classical poetry, scientific journals, journalism
- **Music:** brilliant, clear, clean, light, staccato, bells, flute, violin
- **Sports:** fencing, karate, kyudo
- **Food and drink:** Japanese tea ceremony, Japanese food, nouvelle cuisine, gin and tonics
- **Sound:** *ee*

Concepts, Symbols
- **Wisdom:** mirrorlike
- **Symbol:** scepter
- **Direction in mandala:** east
- **Abilities of mind:** having an overview, facility with logic and reasoning, critical and sharp
- **Concerns:** boundaries, making things right, being disciplined
- **Ways of knowing:** panoramic and detailed
- **Learning style:** intellectual; using analysis, abstractions, and general principles
- **Thinking/language:** clear, orderly, precise; having a big view; often complex and elegant
- **Spiritual style/religion:** philosophical, intellectual
- **Therapeutic approaches:** psychoanalysis, shiatsu

RATNA QUALITIES

Physical Manifestations
- **People:** kings, queens, Jewish mothers, cooks
- **Style of dress:** rich, colorful, lots of ornamentation
- **Sense perceptions:** smell, taste, touch (sensation)
- **Areas of the body:** solar plexus, stomach, skin
- **Health problems:** anorexia, bulimia, addictions
- **Element:** earth
- **Season:** autumn
- **Time of day:** late afternoon
- **Color:** yellow
- **Shape:** square
- **Movement element:** kinesthetics
- **Landscapes/environments:** tropical jungles and dense forests, richly decorated interiors
- **Animals:** elephants, bears, whales, pigs, tropical birds

Expression

- **Passion:** wanting it all
- **Sane activities:** enriching, appreciating the world
- **Neurotic activity:** overindulgence
- **Mode:** quality or texture
- **Style:** overbearing
- **Intensified emotions:** greed and pride fed by poverty mentality
- **Breakdown points:** self-pity, neediness, hunger for more
- **Sense of insufficiency:** feeling inadequate, inferior
- **Defense mechanisms:** arrogance; amassing anything, spiritual or material
- **Realm:** hungry ghost
- **Intensified preoccupation:** wanting to possess
- **Fears:** insubstantiality, not having enough
- **Source of security:** expanding personal territory
- **Relationships:** being the center of attention, possessive
- **Cultures:** Russian and Ottoman empires, Ming dynasty, Slavic, German (Bavarian), Balinese, Greek, Italian, Jewish, American consumerism
- **Art styles:** romantic, baroque, Tibetan, overstuffed rooms and furniture
- **Visual art:** Renaissance, Brueghel, Rubens, happenings
- **Architecture:** massive, solid, elaborate, Roman, baroque, art deco
- **Dance:** ethnic and folk, ritual, court dance, coronations, African, belly dance, contact improvisation
- **Literature:** romantic, elaborate epic novels, Tolstoy, Goethe, Dickens
- **Music:** regal and grand, opera, choral, Wagner, Beethoven, Tchaikovsky, gamelan
- **Sports:** mud wrestling
- **Food and drink:** steak and potatoes with gravy, eggnog
- **Sound:** *ooh*

Concepts, Symbols
- **Wisdom:** equanimity
- **Symbol:** jewel
- **Direction in mandala:** south
- **Ability of mind:** being comprehensive and thorough
- **Concern:** wanting to encompass everything and everyone
- **Way of knowing:** retaining large amounts of information
- **Learning styles:** amassing information, doing research
- **Thinking/language:** thorough, circular, comprehensive, elaborate
- **Spiritual style/religion:** cosmic devotion, awe, prayer, ritualized
- **Therapeutic approaches:** body therapy, Gestalt, family therapy, reparenting, environmental

PADMA QUALITIES

Physical Manifestations
- **People:** people people, performers, therapists, babies, adolescents, sorority sisters
- **Style of dress:** flashy, colorful, sexy
- **Sense perception:** hearing
- **Areas of the body:** mouth, throat, neck, eyes, hands, genitals
- **Health problems:** high blood pressure, insomnia
- **Element:** fire
- **Season:** spring
- **Time of day:** dusk, twilight
- **Color:** red
- **Shape:** half circle
- **Movement elements:** dynamics, rhythm
- **Landscapes/environments:** gardens, flowering meadows, rolling hills; warm, cozy interiors
- **Animals:** butterflies, peacocks, dogs, cats

Expression

- **Passion:** wanting to feel
- **Sane activities:** magnetizing, communicating
- **Neurotic activities:** fantasizing, manipulating
- **Modes:** speech, emotion
- **Style:** intimate
- **Intensified emotions:** clinging passion, comparison to others
- **Breakdown points:** obsession, unfulfilled desires, addiction to intensity
- **Sense of insufficiency:** feeling incomplete, lonely, and depressed
- **Defense mechanism:** desire to please
- **Realm:** human
- **Intensified preoccupation:** insecurity about relationships
- **Fears:** boredom, mediocrity, rejection
- **Sources of security:** making relationships and genuine contact, getting confirmation
- **Relationships:** intimate, sometimes superficial or overly passionate, push-pull dynamic
- **Cultures:** aesthetic, refined, haute couture, southern European, Californian, Hawaiian
- **Art styles:** romantic, expressionist
- **Visual art:** sensuous, colorful, soft
- **Architecture:** homes, nightclubs, resorts
- **Dance:** expressionistic, pas de deux, ballroom, belly dance, striptease
- **Literature:** poetry, novels, magazines, song lyrics
- **Music:** warm, sad, playful, romantic, melodic, lyrical, blues, love songs
- **Sports:** party games
- **Food and drink:** aesthetic presentation, flavorful, exotic
- **Sound:** *e* (eh)

Concepts, Symbols

- **Wisdom:** discriminating awareness
- **Symbol:** lotus

- **Direction in mandala:** west
- **Abilities of mind:** being intuitive, discriminating fine points
- **Concerns:** communication, self-image, pleasure
- **Ways of knowing:** from the heart, intuitive, by association
- **Learning style:** intuitive, using imagery, creative expression, and empathetic communication
- **Thinking/language:** individualistic, intuitive, creative, feeling-based; by association, analogy, metaphor
- **Spiritual style/religion:** devotional, sexual
- **Therapeutic approaches:** group, Gestalt, transactional analysis, sensual massage

KARMA QUALITIES

Physical Manifestations
- **People:** military personnel, laborers, newspaper reporters, workaholics, athletes, dancers, social activists
- **Style of dress:** plain, functional, drab colors
- **Sense perception:** touch (connection)
- **Areas of the body:** limbs
- **Health problems:** high blood pressure
- **Elements:** air, wind
- **Season:** summer
- **Time of day:** morning
- **Color:** green
- **Shape:** triangle
- **Movement element:** kinetics
- **Landscapes/environments:** big, busy cities; functional interiors
- **Animals:** beavers, roadrunners, ants, bees, woodpeckers, hummingbirds

Expression
- **Passion:** wanting to do
- **Sane activity:** creating and carrying out projects

- **Neurotic activity:** driven busyness
- **Mode:** action
- **Style:** direct, straightforward
- **Intensified emotion:** jealousy fed by paranoia and comparison
- **Breakdown point:** overdrive leading to exhaustion, depletion
- **Sense of insufficiency:** feeling incompetent, performance anxiety
- **Defense mechanism:** taking control
- **Realm:** jealous god
- **Intensified preoccupation:** needing to get it done
- **Fear:** failure
- **Source of security:** warding off threats by getting ahead
- **Relationships:** direct and straightforward
- **Cultures:** United States, Japanese, Chinese, Nazi, Stalinist, dominant
- **Art styles:** filmmaking, political art, Mexican murals, graffiti, expressionists
- **Visual art:** de Kooning, Pollock, Escher, pop art, op art, found objects
- **Architecture:** sports centers, train and bus stations, airports
- **Dance:** jazz, aerobics, Jazzercise, rock videos, tap dance, break dancing, African
- **Literature:** adventure stories, political treatises, how-to manuals, cartoons
- **Music:** wrathful, speedy, jumpy, harsh, militant, rap, Penderecki, Stravinsky, Carter, Bartók, Ketjak monkey chant, Talking Heads
- **Sports:** most sports, martial arts
- **Food and drink:** fast food, foraging, coffee, sugar
- **Sound:** *o* (o)

Concepts, Symbols
- **Wisdom:** all-accomplishing
- **Symbol:** sword
- **Direction in mandala:** north
- **Ability of mind:** bringing thought into action without hesitation
- **Concern:** making sure things get done

- **Way of knowing:** seeing how things work
- **Learning styles:** by doing, trial and error
- **Thinking/language:** speedy, matter of fact, pragmatic, could be manipulative
- **Spiritual style/religion:** doing good works, evangelical, techniques, goals
- **Therapeutic approaches:** behavioral therapy, dance therapy, transactional analysis, Rolfing

BUDDHA QUALITIES

Physical Manifestations
- **People:** spiritual teachers, dignified peasants
- **Style of dress:** simple, muted colors
- **Sense perception:** mind (switchboard for five senses)
- **Areas of the body:** back of head, head
- **Health problems:** nonspecific, depends on what other energies are present
- **Element:** space
- **Season:** winter
- **Time of day:** no particular one
- **Color:** white
- **Shape:** circle
- **Movement elements:** space, time
- **Landscapes/environments:** great plains, deserts, and snow fields; sparsely furnished interiors
- **Animals:** owls, cows, whales, polar bears, turtles, jellyfish, camels

Expression
- **Passion:** wanting to just be
- **Sane activity:** just being
- **Neurotic activities:** immobility and dullness
- **Mode:** physical
- **Style:** spacious, minimal, one-pointed

- **Intensified emotions:** ignorance or denial fed by insecurity
- **Breakdown point:** overwhelm coupled with denial and neglect
- **Sense of insufficiency:** not certain who one is
- **Defense mechanisms:** shutting down, tunnel vision
- **Realms:** animal, god
- **Intensified preoccupations:** nose to the ground, absorption
- **Fear:** intrusion
- **Sources of security:** closing down and making things simple
- **Relationships:** spacious, simple
- **Cultures:** simple, tribal, Amish
- **Art styles:** contemplative forms, minimalist
- **Visual art:** minimalist, Japanese brush painting
- **Architecture:** igloos, domes
- **Dance:** whirling dervishes, t'ai chi, American Indian, Japanese court dance
- **Literature:** haiku, minimalist
- **Music:** chanting, overtones, gongs, koto, drums, shakuhachi, Philip Glass, Steve Reich
- **Sports:** fishing
- **Food and drink:** tofu, rice crackers, sake, macrobiotic
- **Sound:** *a* (ah)

Concepts, Symbols
- **Wisdom:** all-pervading space
- **Symbols:** wheel, circle
- **Direction in mandala:** center
- **Ability of mind:** spaciousness
- **Concern:** nondoing
- **Way of knowing:** by just being
- **Learning styles:** repetition using simple, basic concepts; sleeping on it; osmosis
- **Thinking/language:** simple, slow
- **Spiritual style/religion:** meditation, absorption techniques
- **Therapeutic approaches:** client-centered, Rogerian, focused on basic being, breath work, craniosacral

APPENDIX B

Maitri Programs

MAITRI SPACE AWARENESS: FIVE WISDOM ENERGIES PRACTICE

If this book has inspired you to further explore the five energies, you might want to consider attending a Maitri* program, which uses special rooms and postures designed to evoke the energy of each family. Practicing a specified posture for each family in an appropriately colored environment—whether in the Maitri rooms or with colored glasses—is the most direct way to experience the energies.

Each of the rooms is like a box, colored with the energy of its buddha family. You can't be sure what is going to be inside when you open it up. The room can feel like a prison or a sanctuary. Each box is colored and seven feet square, with colored light coming in a specifically shaped window. The buddha room is muted white, with overhead, indirect lighting. The vajra room is deep blue, with narrow horizontal windows. The ratna room is golden yellow, with large circular windows. The padma room is red, with large rectangular windows. The karma room is brilliant green, with green light coming from a square overhead window.

Practicing the posture of the particular family within its room (or

---

*Maitri Space Awareness was developed by Chögyam Trungpa Rinpoche for the use of his students within the Shambhala International community. He also approved the presentation of Maitri Space Awareness in programs for the public presented at the Naropa University and at various contemplative centers that he established. Chögyam Trungpa designed the Maitri rooms and postures for use in the context of Maitri Space Awareness. Since 1994 the Maitri Council International (MCI), under the guidance of Sakyong Mipham Rinpoche, oversees all Mai-

alternatively with colored glasses) penetrates and illuminates our dark corners with a laser beam. Stirring up buried emotions, confusion, and irritation, posture practice holds up a magnifying glass to each nuance of our being. It challenges habitual patterns that might have been locked in our body for years. Because posture practice intensifies whatever pattern it illuminates, we can use this environment to transmute energy readily. By heightening the pattern of energy and surrounding it with maitri, we can transmute it into brilliant sanity. This is the power of practice.

By working with the channels of energy in our bodies, the postures affect our muscles, organs, and glands, which in turn affect our emotions and thoughts. Each posture intensifies and transmutes a specific neurotic pattern by releasing blockages, as follows.

The buddha posture suggests drawing inward, creating a closed, secure place. It works with laziness and a tendency to ignore things—the vast open space behind us. By becoming aware of larger space, we could relax into a sense of basic being.

The vajra posture frustrates the desire to scan our surroundings and take the overview. It thwarts our preoccupation with details. We want to know what is going on and thus become angry. Then we discover that we already know everything we need to know.

The ratna posture has a feeling of expansion. We want to embrace the whole world, but we can't move. We feel there is much more to be appreciated, but the richness is beyond our reach. The posture reinforces a sense of poverty and insubstantiality. At some point we begin to feel the richness inside of us.

The padma posture frustrates the longing to possess something seductive. We can't be easygoing and nice, pleasant and comfortable because we are lying in this posture. We are stuck with mediocrity, even boredom. We discover that our passion is within us and can be self-contained.

---

tri activity. Only teachers authorized by the MCI may teach Maitri using the postures in rooms or with glasses. Anyone can work with the energies.

The karma posture has a rigid immobility that accentuates the tendency to want to move. We become aware of the contrast between moving and not moving. In karma's neurotic state, something always has to be happening; in this restricted state, all we can do is look at the impulse. Eventually we give up the struggle and experience the space.

Generally the postures are done for twenty to forty-five minutes each. Very short sessions—I call them homeopathic doses—have considerable impact for some people; others might need much more intensive practice. The general instruction is to stay with the posture and be present in the room. There is a sense of relaxed firmness to the postures.

The posture practice is followed by fifteen minutes of aimless wandering, in silence, to provide a transition between posture practice and everyday life. It is aimless in the sense that it is without agenda, with no place to go, no one to engage in conversation. Here we begin to notice how the energy of the practice colors our experience of being in the world.

I have been amazed at how often people do a posture briefly, with no idea of what to expect, and then give a textbook description of the energy. On the other hand, people can have a wide range of experiences with each family. There is no particular experience we are meant to have.

Though I have little experience doing this work with children, I'm sure they would "get" the practice immediately. When my daughter was eight, she and I went into the Maitri rooms one day. Though she had seen them before, she was particularly captivated by them this time. Within moments of entering each of the five rooms, we got into its energy. At the end of our half hour, she said, "Now I'm gonna show you the moods we got into in each space." We returned to the rooms, and she did a spontaneous dance in each one. Because she was so open, she had picked up on each energy.

For the most part this practice is very ordinary and should be approached simply. Sitting practice helps by supplying a grounding wire in the form of space for maitri. For that reason we always give equal time to posture practice and sitting practice.

COMMUNITY

Maitri practice is done as an intensive discipline, generally in a group setting. The practice is solitary when using the rooms and done as a group when using the glasses. We practice together for a weekend or longer, creating a nonjudgmental, supportive container with an attitude of fundamental acceptance of whatever arises—in other words, an environment of maitri. It is a safe, nurturing place where we support one another in being genuine. In such a community, we can explore without censure, so our neuroses are neither repressed nor indulged but are openly recognized. It allows the best and the worst to come out. On the one hand, we are free to become caricatures of our neuroses; on the other hand, being kind and helpful to others arises naturally in this environment. External maitri becomes internalized. Practicing in a community makes vivid our interrelatedness. The mandala of interdependence becomes operational.

Creative expression, socializing, playing, and celebrating are encouraged in the group, both spontaneously and as structured events. Programs may include time for energy exploration, an experiential arena in which to express the energies without impulsively acting out or suppressing. Expression makes the energies more vivid, and art disciplines are used to help transmute them. By the end people's moods usually reflect a rich mix of delight, play, appreciation, and humor. That's how I know maitri is happening: melting has been going on.

As a Maitri teacher, each time I face a new group of people, I wonder whether I can possibly feel as close to them, as open with them, as I did with the last group. Each time I do. It's like falling in love again and again and again.

APPENDIX C

Places to Practice Meditation and Maitri

For further information regarding meditation and Maitri programs, please contact one of the following centers.

Karmê Chöling
369 Patneaude Lane
Barnet, VT 05821
U.S.A.
Phone: (802) 633-2384
Web site: *www.kcl.shambhala.org*
E-mail: *karmecholing@shambhala.org*

Rocky Mountain Shambhala Center
4921 County Rd. 68C
Red Feather Lakes, CO 80545-9505
U.S.A.
Phone: (970) 881-2184
Web site: *www.rmsc.shambhala.org*
E-mail: *rmsc@shambhala.org*

Dechen Chöling
Mas Marvent
87700 St. Yrieix sous Aixe
France

Phone: 33 (0)5-55-03-55-52
Web site: *www.shambhala.org/centers/dechen-choling*
E-mail: *dechen-choling@shambhala.org*

Dorje Denma Ling
2280 Balmoral Rd.
Tatamagouche, N.S. B0K 1V0
Canada
Phone: (902) 657-9085
Web site: *www.dorjedenmaling.com*
E-mail: *info@dorjedenmaling.com*

Shambhala International
1084 Tower Rd.
Halifax, N.S. B3H 2Y5
Canada
Phone: (902) 420-1118
Web site: *www.shambhala.org*
E-mail: *info@shambhala.org*

Shambhala Training Europe
Annostrasse 27–33
D-50678 Köln
Germany
Phone: +49 (0221) 31024-01
E-mail: *ste@shambhala.org*

The Maitri Council International is a volunteer organization that promotes and oversees all aspects of Maitri work.
Web site: *www.maitripractice-international.org*

The Five Wisdoms Institute is an international organization that promotes the work of this book. We train, coach/supervise, and facilitate health professionals, educators, organizational leaders, artists, and individuals.

The Five Wisdoms Institute
Irini Rockwell, Director
Phone: (902) 429-4054
Web site: *www.FiveWisdomsInstitute.com*
E-mail: *irinirockwell@shambhala.org*

Naropa University is an accredited, Buddhist-inspired college and graduate school that utilizes Maitri energy work in its approach to contemplative education. For further information about Naropa, write or call:

Naropa University
2130 Arapahoe Ave.
Boulder, CO 80302
U.S.A.
Phone: (303) 444-0202
Web site: *www.naropa.edu*
E-mail: *info@naropa.edu*

The Shambhala Sun is the bimonthly magazine founded by Chögyam Trungpa Rinpoche. Available on newsstands nationwide, it offers genuine Buddhist teachings of all schools and applies the dharma to important issues of modern life.

Shambhala Sun
1585 Barrington St., Suite 300
Halifax, N.S. B3J 1Z8
Canada
Phone: (877) 786-1950 (subscriptions)
Web site: *www.shambhalasun.com*
E-mail: *magazine@shambhalasun.com*

APPENDIX D

Bibliography

Berliner, Helen. *Enlightened by Design.* Boston: Shambhala Publications, 1999.

Chögyam, Ngakpa, with Khandro Dechen. *Spectrum of Ecstasy: Embracing Emotions as the Path of Inner Tantra.* New York and London: Aro Books, 1997. (Previously published as *Rainbow of Liberated Energy: Working with Emotions through the Colour and Element Symbolism of Tibetan Tantra.* Longmead, U.K.: Element Books, 1986.)

Gilkerson, William. *Ultimate Voyage.* Boston: Shambhala Publications, 1999.

Norbu, Thinley. *Magic Dance.* Boston: Shambhala Publications, 1998.

The Tibetan Book of the Dead. Translated with commentary by Francesca Fremantle and Chögyam Trungpa. Boston: Shambhala Publications, 1992.

Trungpa, Chögyam. *Cutting through Spiritual Materialism.* Boston: Shambhala Publications, 1987.

———. *Dharma Art.* Boston: Shambhala Publications, 1996.

———. *Journey without Goal.* Boston: Shambhala Publications, 2000.

———. *The Lion's Roar.* Boston: Shambhala Publications, 1992.

———. *The Myth of Freedom and the Way of Meditation.* Boston: Shambhala Publications, 1998.

———. *Orderly Chaos: The Mandala Principle.* Boston: Shambhala Publications, 1991.

———. *Secret beyond Thought: The Five Chakras and the Four Karmas.* Halifax, N.S., Canada: Vajradhatu Publications, 1991.

———. *Transcending Madness: The Experience of the Six Bardos.* Boston: Shambhala Publications, 1992.

Wegela, Karen Kissel. *How to Be a Help Instead of a Nuisance: Practical Approaches to Giving Support, Service, and Encouragement to Others.* Boston: Shambhala Publications, 1996.

Index